Laches

and

Charmides

ISBN 0-87220-134-1 (paper)

ISBN 0-87220-135-X (cloth)

Originally published in 1973 by
The Library of Liberal Arts

Original Library of Congress
Catalog Card Number 72-86556

PLATO

Laches

and

Charmides

Translated,
with an Introduction
and Notes, by

ROSAMOND KENT SPRAGUE

HACKETT PUBLISHING COMPANY
Indianapolis/Cambridge

Plato: ca. 428–347 B.C.

Copyright © 1992 by Hackett Publishing Company, Inc.

Printed in the United States of America

07 06 05 04 03 02 01   3 4 5 6 7 8

Cover design by Listenberger Design & Associates

Text design by Starr Atkinson

For further information please address
  Hackett Publishing Company, Inc.
  P.O. Box 44937
  Indianapolis, Indiana 46244–0937

Library of Congress Cataloging-in-Publication Data

Plato.
    [Laches. English]
    Laches; and, Charmides/Plato: translated, with an introduction
and notes, by Rosamond Kent Sprague.
        p.   cm.
    Includes bibliographical references and index.
    ISBN 0-87220-135-X: ISBN 0-87220-134-1 (pbk.)
    1. Courage—Early works to 1800. 2. Temperance—Early works to
1800. I. Sprague, Rosamond Kent. II. Plato. Charmides. English.
1992. III. Title: Laches. IV. Title: Charmides.
B373.A5S67 1992
184—dc20   92-6207
                                                    CIP

The paper used in this publication meets the minimum requirements
of American National Standard for Information Sciences—Perma-
nence of Paper for Printed Library Materials, ANSI Z39.48–1984.

♾

Contents

Preface

The *Laches* and *Charmides* are generally agreed to belong to
the group of early Platonic dialogues in which Socrates is
the dominant figure and in which an attempt is made—os-
tensibly unsuccessful—to reach the definition of a single virtue.
Other dialogues close in theme (and presumably also close in
time of composition) are the *Lysis, Euthyphro,* and *Hippias
Major.* In this volume I have placed the *Laches* first as being
simpler than the *Charmides* and as providing a more leisurely
introduction to the Socratic method.

Well-known historical figures play a prominent part in
both dialogues, and we may be sure that Plato expected his
readers to have in mind the subsequent role of Nicias in the
disastrous Sicilian expedition of 415 and the ultimate partici-
pation of Charmides and Critias in the bloody events of 404/3.
To demonstrate that Socrates could not have been the cor-
rupting influence in either case was no doubt part of Plato's
purpose. More positively, his purpose seems also to have been
to show that the best method of defining a virtue is to display
the person who possesses it. In each of the two dialogues,
Socrates' request for the definition of the particular virtue concerned is addressed to a person who might reasonably be expected to have it: the two generals, Laches and Nicias, are
asked to say what courage is, and that remarkably promising
young man, Charmides, is asked to do the same for temperance. In both cases the respondents fail (with the implication
that they therefore do not possess the virtues which they cannot define), but there remains a strong hint in both dialogues
that Socrates has the virtue and is meant to be the answer to
the question what the virtue is. From this point of view neither
dialogue is as inconclusive as it first appears.

This apparent inconclusiveness may well be the greatest difficulty for the student reading the *Laches* and *Charmides* for the first time. In each case a virtue is proposed for definition. Various definitions are then put forward, and each of them is disqualified by Socrates. In the end the entire company, including Socrates himself, declare themselves worsted. Is there any point to this seemingly fruitless procedure? The key to the question is most probably to be found in the nature of Socratic method, as described, for instance, by Plato in the *Apology*. Here we learn (22D) that Socrates considered false conceit of knowledge to be the greatest barrier to human wisdom. A man like Laches, for instance, who is quite confident of knowing what courage is (190E), will not prove receptive to a fresh definition until he is first made to see the contradictory nature of the old one. Hence the necessity for the destructive tactics of the Socratic *elenchus*.[1] So far so good. But are the *Laches* and *Charmides* entirely devoted to *elenchus*? Is nothing positive to be salvaged? Here the answer is much more difficult and can hardly be attempted except on the basis of a detailed study of both dialogues with reference to particular passages. Suffice it to say now that I do believe that both dialogues contain important philosophical points and that a close study of Plato's text will suggest what these are. In the separate introductions and in the notes I have attempted to be more specific.

A word should be said about certain technical terms which I have occasionally employed in the introductions and in the notes.

1) First-order art: an art that possesses a recognizable scope or product, such as carpentry, medicine, or geometry.

2) Second-order art: an art the scope of which comprises arts of the first order, such as rhetoric, sophistry, or statesmanship.

3) *Tinos*—word: (literally, an *"of-what"*-word) a word that appears to be complete but is not, since it demands an-

---

1. The word means cross-examination for the purposes of refutation.

other word or words to explain it. The word "knowledge", for instance, raises the question, knowledge of what?[2]

I have translated Burnet's Oxford Text, by kind permission of the Clarendon Press. Not all of the notes are addressed to the same group of readers; I leave it to the individual's good sense to determine which of them he will find useful. I am indebted to an anonymous reader for his suggestions for revising the translation and to my own university for the sabbatical leave which has enabled me to finish this piece of work.

ROSAMOND KENT SPRAGUE
University of South Carolina

2. I have taken over these terms from my book, *Plato's Philosopher-King: A Study of the Theoretical Background*, published by the University of South Carolina Press. As is there explained, they are intended as a species of shorthand and not as an attempt to impose upon Plato ways of speaking which would be foreign to his thought.

Laches

Introduction

If the reader begins the *Laches* in expectation of a speedy encounter with the cut and thrust of Socratic dialectic, he will find himself disappointed. Socrates does not go into action until 184D (then only briefly), and a first definition of courage is not offered until more than half-way through the dialogue, at 190E. Perhaps, however, it may be useful to think of the opening pages of the *Laches* as an introduction to all dialogues in which Plato deals with the definition of individual virtues and with the question whether virtue can be taught. In other words, if the opening of the *Laches* had not been so lengthy, perhaps the opening of, say, the *Meno,* could not have been so abrupt.

Plato's preoccupation with the nature of virtue and the virtues is a result of his preoccupation with the problem of good government. As Plato saw it, the way to achieve good government is to transfer power to the hands of good men. (To put it in his own way, philosophers must become kings, or kings philosophers.) But how are we to produce these good men? They certainly do not appear spontaneously, so that, as he says in the *Meno* (89B), we could lock them up in the citadel until they were needed by the state. Nor are they the result of heredity, so that we could be sure of finding them among the sons of good men. (See *Laches* 179C and *Meno* 93Cff.) The problem boils down to one of education.

To say that Plato is concerned with education does not mean, however, that he regularly occupies himself in the dialogues with a curriculum for students of virtue. (He does do this in the *Republic,* in Book VII 521Dff.) In earlier dialogues he is more concerned with preliminary questions, such as the following: can virtue in fact be taught? Who are its teachers? What would their credentials be? Ought we to decide what virtue is before deciding whether it can be taught? Could we

3

educate a man in one of the virtues apart from educating him
in all? Is virtue a subject of the same sort as other techniques
or arts? What is the relationship between virtue and knowledge? Or between possessing a virtue and being able to define
it? If the *Laches* is read as an examination of questions like
these, it can be seen as having close links not only with the
Charmides but with the *Apology, Crito, Protagoras* and *Meno.*

The subsidiary characters Lysimachus and Melesias have
not only a positive but also a familiar function, for instance.
At 179C we learn that they are the undistinguished sons of distinguished fathers. The interesting thing about them is that
they should recognize this themselves and that they should
seek to reverse the situation by at least giving close attention
to the education of their own sons. In this they show correct
Socratic ignorance (not thinking they know things that they
do not know), and they have the correct idea that those who
are ignorant should seek the advice of experts. They have decided to consult Nicias and Laches, not, be it noted, because
they are military men (and so might reasonably be expected
to pass an informed judgment on the value of learning to
fight in armor), but because they are *parents* (179B and 187C)
and must also have given consideration to the problem of educating young men. When Laches suggests (180B) that Socrates
would be much more of an expert than either himself or
Nicias, Lysimachus is quite ready to consult Socrates instead.
We may say that Lysimachus is uncritical in his choice of
experts (he has brought Nicias and Laches to the military
show on the advice of an unnamed "somebody" 179E), but at
least he and Melesias have the right basic notions: that the
education of the young is an important matter, that he and
Melesias are unfitted for the task themselves, and that expert
advice must be sought. When the experts disagree, however,
Lysimachus is more or less at a loss. He can only suggest that
Socrates should cast the deciding vote (184CD).

It is this suggestion of majority rule which really brings
Socrates onto the field. Decisions, he says (184E), should be
made by knowledge, not by numbers. Hence we ought to try

to determine which persons possess the knowledge we need—who really are the experts, in other words. Of course, we shall want those who have studied and practised and who have had good teachers. But we also need to be clear about what we want them to be experts *in* (185B). This point (which will lead ultimately to the distinction between first- and second-order arts both here and, more conspicuously, in the *Charmides*) produces, first, an important observation on the relationship of means to ends (185CD) and then an announcement that the real topic of inquiry is not the art of fighting in armor but the souls of young men (185DE). Once we are clear about what we are investigating, we can reopen the question of experts and their credentials. Is any one of us expert in the care of the soul? Again he must have had good teachers (in the *Meno* we are asked to consider who these might be) or failing that, he must produce well-executed products (185E). The analogy with the first-order arts is consistently maintained; where the expert sculptor would, presumably, exhibit a good statue, the expert in the soul would need to exhibit a good man. Socrates will not admit to meeting either requirement, of having had good teachers or of having found out the art for himself (186BC).

An impasse has now been reached, and some fresh approach is needed to get the discussion going again. This is outlined by Socrates at 189Eff. and more clearly stated at 190B, where he says:

> Then isn't it necessary for us to start out knowing what virtue is? Because if we are not absolutely certain what it is, how are we going to advise anyone as to the best method of obtaining it?

The remainder of the dialogue consists of attempts to say what at least one of the virtues is. We find out, in the process, that the isolation of courage, methodologically useful as it may appear (190C), is not a successful move, since if courage is some species of knowledge, it can hardly be distinguished from any other virtue. (Here we have adumbrations of the identification of temperance with knowledge in the *Charmides* and of the whole question of the unity of the virtues canvassed in the *Protagoras*).

The student will no doubt be able to identify the various definitions of courage as they appear and to follow out the course of the various refutations, and it ought to be superfluous to suggest that there is much to be gained from the performance of this obvious task. A less obvious point for him to consider is this: why is the dialogue called *Laches?* It has been eloquently argued that the two generals represent the familiar Greek contrast between *logos* and *ergon,* with Nicias representing thought and Laches action.[1] Laches does appear to be a bluff soldier type, offering a soldier's view of courage and admiring Socrates less for his intellect than for his exploits in the field. Nicias, on the other hand, seems to have had more experience in philosophical discussion and to be more closely acquainted with the methods of Socrates. I would argue, however, that the dialogue is called *Laches* because Laches shows a more promising reaction to the Socratic *elenchus* than does Nicias.

To clarify this point it will be useful to refer again to the presumably later dialogue *Meno.* Here we have an interesting episode in which Socrates attempts to demonstrate that knowledge is recollection. He proceeds to lead an uninstructed slave boy through the steps of a geometrical proof, not by means of instruction, but by means of questions. The details of the proof are relatively unimportant: the point to note is that the boy progresses through a well-defined series of attitudes with respect to his own knowledge. First he is confident that he knows the answer (a wrong answer), then he comes to the realization of his own ignorance, then he makes a fresh start and reaches the right answer. A parallel course is followed by Meno with respect to the problem of the definition of virtue, but through the first two stages only. By his obstinate

1. See Michael J. O'Brien, "The Unity of the *Laches,*" *Yale Classical Studies* XVIII (1963) : 133-147.

refusal to take things in the correct order, he never reaches a satisfactory conclusion.

If we look at the progress of Laches from this point of view, the comparison is instructive. When Socrates first asks him what the definition of courage is, he is full of confidence (190E). But after the second attempt (which is, incidentally, a great improvement over the first) he comes to a realization of his own ignorance (193D). The really interesting thing about Laches is his reaction to this discovery: He says

> I am ready not to give up, Socrates, although I am not really accustomed to arguments of this kind. But an absolute desire for victory has seized me with respect to our conversation, and I am really getting annoyed at being unable to express what I think in this fashion. I still think I know what courage is, but I can't understand how it has escaped me just now so that I can't pin it down in words and say what it is. (194AB).

This speech of Laches' recalls a passage in the later dialogue *Theaetetus,* where Plato describes the reaction which a dialectician may hope for from his respondent:

> . . . your companion will lay the blame of his own confusion and perplexity on himself, and not on you. He will follow and love you, and will hate himself, and escape from himself into philosophy, in order that he may become different and be quit of his former self. 168A (trans. Jowett).

This is, in essence, the effect which the Socratic *elenchus* has had upon Laches. Earlier he has presented himself to Socrates as someone for him to teach and to refute in any way he pleases; his only stipulation in learning is that his teacher shall be good (189AB). Later he has made sufficient progress to initiate a brief Socratic discussion himself (195BC and cf. 195E), an unusual undertaking (we may compare Cleinias at *Euthydemus* 290Bff.) and one which earns the approval of

Socrates. This is about his furthest limit, however, and the rest of the dialogue finds him withdrawing in favor of Socrates and indulging in a certain amount of backbiting and sarcasm at the expense of Nicias. He still retains his conviction of ignorance, however, and the end of the dialogue finds him still declining to accept the role of instructor of the young (200C).

Nicias presents a much more complex picture. His speech in favor of the art of fighting in armor is flat in comparison with the energetic attack on the art by Laches. Later in the dialogue, however, he shows greater intellectual power, as well as being able to follow Laches' example in taking the discussion briefly into his own hands (195D). He claims fairly extensive acquaintance with the methods of Socrates (187Dff.), but at one point he asks a question that is naive if this acquaintance is at all thorough (185C). He can repeat one of the basic Socratic doctrines ("every one of us is good with respect to that in which he is wise and bad in respect to that in which he is ignorant" 194D) and seems to understand what some of its important implications are. But although in the end he agrees with Laches that Socrates, if he can be persuaded, would be the best teacher for the boys, he seems no less satisfied with his own intellectual state than he was in the beginning. There may be a few troublesome points to settle, but this will be easily done with the help of Damon and others. His final speech to Laches is made from the kindly heights of self-satisfaction:

> "And when I feel secure on these points, I will instruct you too and won't begrudge the effort—because you seem to me to be sadly in need of learning." (200B)

I think Plato means us to feel that whereas Nicias may be the more gifted, his philosophical progress will be less than that of Laches since it is unlikely that he will ever be made to feel angry with himself. Hence I believe that *Laches* is the right title for the dialogue. The reader will, however, want to form his own opinion on this point.

Persons of the "Laches"

Lysimachus is the son of Aristides the Just and is mentioned by Demosthenes (*Against Leptinus* 115) as having received a considerable state pension of land and money. At *Meno* 94A he suffers in comparison with his distinguished father.

Melesias, who on one occasion served as an envoy of the Four Hundred (Thucydides VIII, 86, 9) is the son of Thucydides the general. At *Meno* 94C Socrates says that Thucydides had his two sons trained to be the best wrestlers in Athens, but implies that he failed to teach them virtue.

Boys are the two sons of Lysimachus and Melesias, who are named after their distinguished grandparents (179A). They speak but once in the dialogue (181A).

Nicias (ca. 470-413) is a distinguished statesman and general who was the principal rival of Cleon in the period following the death of Pericles (see Aristophanes, *Knights*). He negotiated the so-called Peace of Nicias with Sparta in 421 and was an opponent of the ill-fated Syracusan expedition of 415. In spite of his opposition to the expedition he was, together with Lamachus and Alcibiades, put in charge of it. It seems clear from Thucydides' account (Books VI and VII) that it was his overcautious and superstitious behavior that led to the Athenian disaster. (See also Plutarch, *Nicias*.)

Laches, son of Melanopus, is also a general but less distinguished than Nicias. Thucydides reports (III, 86, 1) that in 427 he and Charoeades were sent to Sicily with twenty ships to assist Leontini against Syracuse. Later (III, 90, 2ff.) Laches secured the surrender of the Messenians. He was with Socrates in the retreat from Delium of 424 where, according to Plato (*Symposium* 221AB), it was Socrates who showed the superior courage. (See also *Laches* 181B and 189B). He supported Nicias in the negotiations leading to the Peace of 421 and fell at the battle of Mantinaea in 418. In Aristophanes' *Wasps* he makes an entertaining appearance as a dog, Labes, prosecuted by another dog, Kuōn (Cleon). See 835ff. and 891ff.

Socrates is about fifty years old at the time of the dialogue.

Dramatic Date

The dramatic date is roughly determined for us by Laches' mention (181B) of the retreat from Delium of 424 and by his own death in the battle of Mantinaea in 418. To date the conversation any more precisely (to say, for instance, whether Plato imagines it to have taken place before or after the Peace of Nicias in 421) is probably not possible, nor is it particularly necessary.

Selected Bibliography

BUFORD, THOMAS O. "Plato on the Educational Consultant: An Interpretation of the *Laches.*" *Idealistic Studies* VII. 1977. Pp. 151–171.

BURNET, JOHN, ed. *Platonis Opera,* vol. 3. "Oxford Classical Texts." Oxford, 1903. Reprinted 1957.

CROISET, ALFRED, ed. *Lachès,* in "Collection des Universités de France." Budé Edition, vol. 2. Paris, 1965.

DE LAGUNA, THEODORE. "The Problem of the Laches," in *Mind* XLIII (1934): 170–180.

DEVEREUX, DANIEL T. "Courage and Wisdom in Plato's *Laches.*" *Journal of the History of Philosophy* XV, 2. 1977. Pp. 129–141.

FRIEDLÄNDER, PAUL. *Plato: The Dialogues (First Period).* Translated by Hans Meyerhoff. New York, 1964. Pp. 38–49.

GUTHRIE, W. K. C. *A History of Greek Philosophy* IV. Cambridge: Cambridge, 1975. Pp. 124–134.

HOERBER, ROBERT G. "Plato's *Laches,*" in *Classical Philology* LXIII, 2 (1968): 95–105.

KAHN, CHARLES H. "Plato on the Unity of the Virtues." *Facets of Plato's Philosophy.* ed. W. H. Werkmeister. Amsterdam: 1976.

LANE, IAIN. Translation with introduction and notes. *Early Socratic Dialogues.* ed. Trevor J. Saunders. New York: *Penguin Classics,* 1987.

O'BRIEN, MICHAEL J. "The Unity of the *Laches,*" in *Yale Classical Studies,* vol. 18. New Haven, 1963. Pp. 133–147.

PLAISTOWE, F. G., and Mills, T. R., eds. *Plato: "Laches",* London [n.d.]

SANTAS, GERASIMOS. "Socrates at Work on Virtue and Knowledge in Plato's *Laches,*" in *Review of Metaphysics* XXII, 3 (1969): 433–460.

SHOREY, PAUL. *What Plato Said.* Chicago, 1933. Pp. 106–112.

STOKES, MICHAEL V. *Plato's Socratic Conversations: Drama and Dialectic in the Three Middle Dialogues.* Baltimore: Johns Hopkins, 1986. Chapter II.

TATHAM, M. T., ed. *"The Laches" of Plato.* London, 1891.

TAYLOR, A. E. *Plato: The Man and His Work.* London, 1926. (6th edition reprinted 1949) Pp. 57–64.

TELOH, HENRY. *Socratic Education in Plato's Early Dialogues.* Notre Dame, Indiana: Notre Dame, 1986. Chapter III. "Character and Education in the *Laches.*"

VICAIRE, PAUL, ed. *Platon: Lachès et Lysis,* in "Collection de Textes Grecs Commentés." Paris, 1963.

Laches

LYSIMACHUS   You have seen the man fighting in armor,   178A
Nicias and Laches.[1] When Melesias and I invited you to see
him with us, we neglected to give the reason why, but now we
shall explain, because we think it especially right to be frank
with you. Now there are some people who make fun of frankness and if anyone asks their advice, they don't say what   B
they think, but they make a shot at what the other man would
like to hear and say something different from their own opinion. But you we considered capable not only of forming a
judgment but also, having formed one, of saying exactly what
you think, and this is why we have taken you into our confidence about what we are going to communicate to you. Now
the matter about which I have been making such a long pre-   179A
amble is this: we have these two sons here—this one is the
son of my friend Melesias here, and he is called Thucydides
after his grandfather, and this one is my son, who also goes
by his grandfather's name—we call him Aristides after my
father.[2] We have made up our minds to take as good care
of them as we possibly can and not to behave like most parents, who, when their children start to grow up, permit them
to do whatever they wish. No, we think that now is the time to

---

1. Plato sometimes likes to begin a dialogue at the point where a
professional display has ended. Cf. the *Gorgias, Hippias Minor,* and (with
a greater lapse of time between display and dialogue) *Ion.* For another
reference to displays of fighting in armor, see *Euthydemus* 271D. The two
elderly sophists, Euthydemus and Dionysodorus, have, however, abandoned
fighting in armor for fighting with words.
2. To name the grandson after the grandfather was a fairly general
Athenian custom.

179B make a real beginning, so far as we can. Since we knew that both of you had sons too, we thought that you, if anyone, would have been concerned about the sort of training that would make the best men of them. And if by any chance you have not turned your attention to this kind of thing very often, let us remind you that you ought not to neglect it, and let us invite you to care for your sons along with ours.[3] How we reached this conclusion, Nicias and Laches, you must hear, even if it means my talking a bit longer. Now you must know

C that Melesias and I take our meals together, and the boys eat with us. We shall be frank with you, exactly as I said in the beginning: each of us has a great many fine things to say to the young men about his own father, things they achieved both in war and in peace in their management of the affairs both of their allies and of the city here. But neither of us has a word to say about his own accomplishments. This is what shames us

D in front of them, and we blame our fathers for allowing us to take things easy when we were growing up, while they were busy with other peoples' affairs. And we point these same things out to the young people here, saying that if they are careless of themselves and disobedient to us, they will turn out to be nobodies, but if they take pains, perhaps they may become worthy of the names they bear.[4] Now the boys promise to be obedient, so we are looking into the question what form of instruction or practise would make them turn out best.

E Somebody suggested this form of instruction to us, saying that it would be a fine thing for a young man to learn fighting in

---

3. Nothing appears to be known of any son of Laches. Nicias' son, Niceratus (mentioned below at 200D), was put to death by the Thirty. (See Xenophon *Hellenica* II, 3, 39 and *Diodorus Siculus* XIV, 5, 5.) As to his education, we learn from Xenophon *Symposium* III, 5 that his father had him memorize all of Homer. He even seems to have competed as a rhapsode, according to Aristotle *Rhetoric* 1413a7ff. He is present as an auditor in the *Republic* (327C).

4. Concerning the boys' future we know nothing except what Plato tells us of Aristides at *Theaetetus* 150Eff.: that he became an associate of Socrates but left his company too soon. (Cf. the passage in the pseudo-Platonic *Theages* 130Aff. in which both Aristides and the young Thucydides are mentioned.)

armor. And he praised this particular man whom you have just seen giving a display and proceeded to encourage us to see him. So we thought we ought to go to see the man and to take you with us, not only as fellow-spectators but also as fellow-counsellors and partners, if you should be willing, in the care of our sons. This is what we wanted to share with you. So now is the time for you to give us your advice, not only about this form of instruction—whether you think it should be learned or not—but also about any other sort of study or pursuit for a young man which you admire. Tell us too, what part you will take in our joint enterprise.

180A

NICIAS   I, for one, Lysimachus and Melesias, applaud your plan and am ready to take part in it. And I think Laches here is ready too.

LACHES   You are quite right, Nicias. As for what Lysimachus said just now about his father and Melesias' father, I think that what he said applied very well to them and to us and to everyone engaged in public affairs, because this is pretty generally what happens to them—that they neglect their private affairs, children as well as everything else, and manage them carelessly. So you were right on this point, Lysimachus. But I am astonished that you are inviting us to be your fellow-counsellors in the education of the young men and are not inviting Socrates here! In the first place, he comes from your own deme,[5] and in the second, he is always spending his time in places where the young men engage in any study or noble pursuit of the sort you are looking for.[6]

B

C

LYSIMACHUS   What do you mean, Laches? Has our friend Socrates concerned himself with any things of this kind?

LACHES   Certainly, Lysimachus.

NICIAS   This is a point I can vouch for no less than

5. Socrates' own deme (or parish) is Alopece, as we learn from *Gorgias* 495D.

6. So, for instance, we find Socrates in the palaestras (wrestling-schools) in the *Lysis* and *Charmides,* and at the Lyceum in the *Euthydemus.* At *Euthyphro* 2A it is thought notable that he is *not* at the Lyceum.

Laches, since he only recently recommended a man to me as
music teacher for my son. The man's name is Damon,[7] a pupil
of Agathocles,[8] and he is the most accomplished of men, not
only in music, but in all the other pursuits in which you would
think it worthwhile for boys of his age to spend their time.

LYSIMACHUS People at my time of life, Socrates, Nicias,
and Laches, are no longer familiar with the young because our
advancing years keep us at home so much of the time. But if
you, son of Sophroniscus, have any good advice to give your
fellow-demesman, you ought to give it. And you have a duty
to do so, because you are my friend through your father. He
and I were always comrades and friends, and he died without our ever having had a single difference. And this present
conversation reminds me of something—when the boys here
are talking to each other at home, they often mention Socrates
and praise him highly, but I've never thought to ask if they
were speaking of the son of Sophroniscus. Tell me, boys, is this
the Socrates you spoke of on those occasions?

BOYS Certainly, father, this is the one.

LYSIMACHUS I am delighted, Socrates, that you keep up
your father's good reputation, for he was the best of men, and
I am especially pleased at the idea that the close ties between
your family and mine will be renewed.

LACHES Don't under any circumstances let the man get
away, Lysimachus—because I have seen him elsewhere keep-

---

7. Damon was a musical theorist and politician and perhaps a sophist.
He was the pupil of both Agathocles and Prodicus (see below 197D) and
the teacher, with Anaxagoras, of Pericles. (See Isocrates *Antidosis* 235 and
Plutarch *Pericles* 4). Plato mentions him, with seeming approval, at
Republic 400B and 424C. See also Diels-Kranz, *Die Fragmente der Vorso-
kratiker* § 37, and, for a balanced account of his relationship to Plato,
Warren D. Anderson, *Ethos and Education in Greek Music* (Cambridge,
Mass., 1966), especially pp. 74-81. To be recommended by Socrates is
certainly an unusual honor.

8. Agathocles was also one of the teachers of Pindar. He is mentioned
by Plato at *Protagoras* 316E as *pretending* to be a musician, although he
was really a sophist.

ing up not only his father's reputation but that of his country. He marched with me in the retreat from Delium,[9] and I can tell you that if the rest had been willing to behave in the same manner, our city would be safe and we would not then have suffered a disaster of that kind.

LYSIMACHUS Socrates, the praise you are receiving is certainly of a high order, both because it comes from men who are to be trusted and because of the qualities for which they praise you. Be assured that I am delighted to hear that you are held in such esteem, and please consider me among those most kindly disposed towards you. You yourself ought to have visited us long before and considered us your friends—that would have been the right thing to do. Well, since we have recognized each other, resolve now, starting today, to associate both with us and the young men here and to make our acquaintance, so that you may preserve the family friendship. So do what I ask, and we in turn shall keep you in mind of your promise. But what have you all to say about our original question? What is your opinion? Is fighting in armor a useful subject for young men to learn or not?

SOCRATES Well, I shall try to advise you about these things as best I can, Lysimachus, in addition to performing all the things to which you call my attention. However, it seems to me to be more suitable, since I am younger than the others and more inexperienced in these matters, for me to listen first to what they have to say and to learn from them. But if I should have something to add to what they say, then will be the time for me to teach and persuade both you and the others. Come, Nicias, why doesn't one of you two begin?

NICIAS Well, there is no reason why not, Socrates. I think that knowledge of this branch of study is beneficial for the young in all sorts of ways. For one thing, it is a good idea

181B

C

D

E

9. The Athenians were defeated by the Boeotians under Pagondas at Delium in November of 424, the eighth year of the Peloponnesian War. Alcibiades refers to the conduct of Socrates in the retreat (to the detriment of Laches) at *Symposium* 220Eff. See also *Apology* 28E and, for an account of the battle, Thucydides IV, 91-96.

for the young not to spend their time in the pursuits in which they normally do like to spend it when they are at leisure, but **182A** rather in this one, which necessarily improves their bodies, since it is in no way inferior to gymnastic exercises and no less strenuous, and, at the same time, this and horsemanship are forms of exercise especially suited to a free citizen. For in the contest in which we are the contestants and in the matters on which our struggle depends,[10] only those are practised who know how to use the instruments of war. And again, there is a certain advantage in this form of instruction even in an actual battle, whenever one has to fight in line with a number of others.[11] But the greatest advantage of it comes when the ranks are broken and it then becomes necessary for **B** a man to fight in single combat, either in pursuit when he has to attack a man who is defending himself, or in flight, when he has to defend himself against another person who is attacking him. A man who has this skill would suffer no harm at the hands of a single opponent, nor even perhaps at the hands of a larger number, but he would have the advantage in every way. Then again, such a study arouses in us the desire for another fine form of instruction, since every man who learns to fight in armor will want to learn the subject that comes next, that is, the science of tactics; and when he has **C** mastered this and taken pride in it, he will press on to the whole art of the general. So it has already become clear that what is connected with this latter art, all the studies and pursuits which are fine and of great value for a man to learn and to practise, have this study as a starting-point.[12] And we shall add to this an advantage which is not at all negligible, that this knowledge will make every man much bolder and braver

10. Nicias presumably refers to the Peloponnesian War.

11. For a good account of Greek warfare, see F. E. Adcock, *The Greek and Macedonian Art of War* (Berkeley and Los Angeles, 1957).

12. It looks as though Nicias were attempting to establish generalship as a science of sciences. That Plato would not agree can be seen from the *Charmides* (this distinction is reserved for the knowledge of good and evil), *Euthydemus* 290Bff., *Ion* 540Eff., and *Statesman* 304Eff.

in war than he was before. And let us not omit to mention, even if to some it might seem a point not worth making, that this art will give a man a finer-looking appearance at the very moment when he needs to have it, and when he will appear   **182D** more frightening to the enemy because of the way he looks. So my opinion, Lysimachus, is just as I say, that young men should be taught these things, and I have given the reasons why I think so. But if Laches has anything to say on the other side, I would be glad to hear it.

LACHES   But the fact is, Nicias, that it is difficult to maintain of any study whatsoever that it ought not to be learned, because it seems to be a good idea to learn everything. So as far as this fighting in armor is concerned, if it is a genu-   **E** ine branch of study, as those who teach it claim, and as Nicias says, then it ought to be learned, but if it is not a real subject and the people who propose to teach it are deceiving us, or if it is a real subject but not a very important one, what need is there to learn it?[13] The reason I say these things about it is that I consider that, if there were anything in it, it would not have escaped the attention of the Lacedaemonians, who have no other concern in life than to look for and engage in what- ever studies and pursuits will increase their superiority in war.   **183A** And if the Lacedaemonians had overlooked the art, the teachers of it would certainly not have overlooked this fact, that the Lacedaemonians are the most concerned with such matters of any of the Greeks and that anyone who was hon- ored among them in these matters would make a great deal of money just as is the case when a tragic poet is honored among us. The result is that whenever anyone fancies himself as a good writer of tragedy, he does not go about exhibiting his   **B** plays in the other cities round about Athens but comes straight here and shows his work to our people, as is the natural thing to do. But I observe that those who fight in armor regard

---

13. Laches shows that he can make a clear analysis of the point at issue, and, just below, he invokes the opinion of the expert—a good Socratic procedure.

Lacedaemon as forbidden ground and keep from setting foot in it. They give it a wide berth and prefer to exhibit to anyone rather than the Spartans—in fact they take pains to select people who themselves admit that plenty of others surpass them 183C in warfare. Then again, Lysimachus, I have encountered quite a few of these gentlemen on the actual field of battle and I have seen what they are like. This makes it possible for us to consider the matter at first hand. In a manner which seems almost deliberate, not a single practitioner of the art of fighting in armor has ever become renowned in war. And yet in all the other arts, those who are well-known in each are those who have practised the various ones. But the men who practise this art seem to be those who have the worst luck at it. For instance, this very man Stesilaus, whom you and I have witnessed D giving a display before such a large crowd and praising himself the way he did, I once saw in the quite different circumstances of actual warfare giving a much finer demonstration against his will. On an occasion when a ship on which he was serving as a marine[14] rammed a transport-vessel, he was armed with a combination scythe and spear, as singular a weapon as he was singular a man. His other peculiarities are not worth relating, but let me tell you how his invention of a scythe plus E a spear turned out. In the course of the fight it somehow got entangled in the rigging of the other ship and there it stuck. So Stesilaus dragged at the weapon in an attempt to free it, but he could not, and meanwhile his ship was going by the other ship. For a time he kept running along the deck holding fast to the spear. But when the other ship was actually passing his and was dragging him after it while he still held onto the 184A weapon, he let it slide through his hand until he just had hold of the ferule at the end. There was laughter and applause from the men on the transport at the sight of him, and when somebody hit the deck at his feet with a stone and he let go the shaft, then even the men on the trireme could no longer keep from laughing when they saw that remarkable scythe-

---

14. That is, as a hoplite on a trireme.

spear dangling from the transport. Now perhaps these things may be of value, as Nicias maintains, but my own experience has been of the sort I describe. So, as I said in the beginning, either it is an art but has little value, or it is not an art but people say and pretend that it is, but in any case it is not worth trying to learn. And then it seems to me that if a cowardly man should imagine he had mastered the art, he would, because of his increasing rashness, show up more clearly the sort of man he was, whereas in the case of a brave man, everyone would be watching him and if he made the smallest mistake, he would incur a great deal of criticism. The reason for this is that a man who pretends to knowledge of this sort is the object of envy, so that unless he is outstandingly superior to the rest, there is no way in which he can possibly avoid becoming a laughingstock when he claims to have this knowledge. So the study of this art seems to me to be of this sort, Lysimachus. But, as I said before, we ought not to let Socrates here escape, but we ought to consult him as to his opinion on the matter in hand.

LYSIMACHUS   Well, I do ask your opinion, Socrates, since what might be called our council seems to me to be still in need of someone to cast the deciding vote. If these two had agreed, there would be less necessity of such a procedure, but as it is, you perceive that Laches has voted in opposition to Nicias. So we would do well to hear from you too, and find out with which of them you plan to vote.

SOCRATES   What's that, Lysimachus? Do you intend to cast your vote for whatever position is approved by the majority of us?[15]

LYSIMACHUS   Why, what else could a person do, Socrates?

SOCRATES   And do you, Melesias, plan to act in the same way? Suppose there should be a council to decide whether your

184B

C

D

E

15. Socrates now makes his first decisive entry into the conversation and does so by preparing the ground for a typically Socratic point: we should accept the opinion of the expert, not that of the majority. Cf. *Crito* 47Aff.

son ought to practise a particular kind of gymnastic exercise, would you be persuaded by the greater number or by whoever has been educated and exercised under a good trainer?

MELESIAS   Probably by the latter, Socrates.

SOCRATES   And you would be persuaded by him rather than by the four of us?

MELESIAS   Probably.

SOCRATES   So I think it is by knowledge that one ought to make decisions, if one is to make them well, and not by majority rule.

MELESIAS   Certainly.

SOCRATES   So in this present case it is also necessary to investigate first of all whether any one of us is an expert in
185A   the subject we are debating, or not. And if one of us is, then we should listen to him even if he is only one, and disregard the others. But if no one of us is an expert, then we must look for someone who is. Or do you and Lysimachus suppose that the subject in question is some small thing and not the greatest of all our possessions? The question is really, I suppose, that of whether your sons turn out to be worthwhile persons or the opposite—and the father's whole estate will be managed in accordance with the way the sons turn out.

MELESIAS   You are right.

SOCRATES   So we ought to exercise great forethought in the matter.

MELESIAS   Yes, we should.

B   SOCRATES   Then, in keeping with what I said just now, how would we investigate if we wanted to find out which of us was the most expert with regard to gymnastics? Wouldn't it be the man who had studied and practised the art and who had had good teachers in that particular subject?

MELESIAS   I should think so.

SOCRATES   And even before that, oughtn't we to investigate what art it is of which we are looking for the teachers?

MELESIAS   What do you mean?

SOCRATES   Perhaps it will be more clear if I put it this way: I do not think we have reached any preliminary agreement as to what in the world we are consulting about and investigating when we ask which of us is expert in it and has acquired teachers for this purpose, and which of us is not.   185C

NICIAS   But, Socrates, aren't we investigating the art of fighting in armor and discussing whether young men ought to learn it or not?[16]

SOCRATES   Quite so, Nicias. But when a man considers whether or not he should use a certain medicine to anoint his eyes, do you think he is at that moment taking counsel about the medicine or about the eyes?[17]

NICIAS   About the eyes.

SOCRATES   Then too, whenever a man considers whether   D
or not and when he should put a bridle on a horse, I suppose he is at that moment taking counsel about the horse and not about the bridle?

NICIAS   That is true.

SOCRATES   So, in a word, whenever a man considers a thing for the sake of another thing, he is taking counsel about that thing for the sake of which he was considering, and not about what he was investigating for the sake of something else.

NICIAS   Necessarily so.

SOCRATES   Then the question we ought to ask with respect to the man who gives us advice, is whether he is expert in the care of that thing for the sake of which we are considering when we consider.

NICIAS   Certainly.

SOCRATES   So do we now declare that we are considering   E
a form of study for the sake of the souls of young men?[18]

16. Since Nicias claims later on (187Dff.) to be an old hand at Socratic discussions, it is somewhat surprising to find him unprepared for this shift from the study of a particular art to the education of the whole man.

17. The argument now follows a typical Socratic pattern: a series of illustrations (here only two) are used to establish a general principle. The general principle is then applied to the particular point at issue (185D). For the primacy of ends over means cf. *Lysis* 218Dff. and *Gorgias* 457Cff.

18. Socrates has now succeeded in shifting the discussion a) from means to ends, b) from bodily training to care of the soul.

NICIAS   Yes.

SOCRATES   Then the question whether any one of us is expert in the care of the soul and is capable of caring for it well, and has had good teachers, is the one we ought to investigate.

LACHES   What's that, Socrates? Haven't you ever noticed that in some matters people become more expert without teachers than with them?

SOCRATES   Yes, I have, Laches, but you would not want to trust them when they said they were good craftsmen unless they should have some well-executed product of their art to show you—and not just one but more than one.

186A

LACHES   What you say is true.

SOCRATES   Then what we ought to do, Laches and Nicias, since Lysimachus and Melesias called us in to give them advice about their two sons out of a desire that the boys' souls should become as good as possible—if we say we have teachers to show, is to point out to them the ones who in the first place are good themselves and have tended the souls of many young men, and in the second place have manifestly taught us. Or, if any one of us says that he himself has had no teacher but has works of his own to tell of, then he ought to show which of the Athenians or foreigners, whether slave or free, is recognized to have become good through his influence.[19] But if this is not the case with any of us, we should give orders that a search be made for others and should not run the risk of ruining the sons of our friends and thus incurring the greatest reproach from their nearest relatives. Now I, Lysimachus and Melesias, am the first to say, concerning myself, that I have had no teacher in this subject. And yet I have longed after it from my youth up. But I did not have any money to give the sophists, who were the only ones who professed to be able to make a cultivated man of me, and I myself, on the other hand, am unable to discover the art even now. If Nicias or Laches

B

C

---

19. Cf. *Gorgias* 514Aff. and note, in both passages, the possibility that a slave might become good.

had discovered it or learned it, I would not be surprised, because they are richer than I and so may have learned it from
others, and also older, so they may have discovered it already.
Thus they seem to me to be capable of educating a man,   186D
because they would never have given their opinions so fear-
lessly on the subject of pursuits which are beneficial and harmful for the young if they had not believed themselves to be
sufficiently informed on the subject. In other matters I have
confidence in them, but that they should differ with each other
surprises me. So I make this counter-request of you, Lysimachus: just as Laches was urging you just now not to let me
go but to ask me questions, so I now call on you not to let
Laches go, or Nicias, but to question them, saying that Socrates denies having any knowledge of the matter or being compe-   E
tent to decide which of you speaks the truth, because he denies
having been a discoverer of such things or having been anyone's pupil in them. So, Laches and Nicias, each of you tell us
who is the cleverest person with whom you have associated in
this matter of educating young men, and whether you acquired
your knowledge of the art from another person or found it out
for yourselves,[20] and, if you learned it from some one, who
were your respective teachers, and what other persons share the   187A
same art with them. My reason for saying all this is that, if you
are too busy because of your civic responsibilities, we can go to
these men and persuade them, either by means of gifts or fa-
vors or both, to look after both our boys and yours too so that
they won't put their ancestors to shame by turning out to be
worthless. But if you yourselves have been the discoverers of
such an art, give us an example of what other persons you
have already made into fine men by your care when they
were originally worthless. Because if you are about to begin
educating people now for the first time, you ought to watch   B
out in case the risk is being run, not by a guinea-pig,[21] but by

20. Cf. *Euthydemus* 285A.
21. Literally, to "try it on the Carian", i.e., some worthless person.
(The Carians often served as mercenaries and would be regarded as less
valuable than the regular citizen soldiers.) Cf. *Euthydemus* 285BC.

your own sons and the children of your friends, and you should keep from doing just what the proverb says not to do— to begin pottery on a wine jar.[22] So state which of these alternatives you would select as being appropriate and fitting for you and which you would reject. Find out these things from them, Lysimachus, and don't let the men escape.

LYSIMACHUS   I like what Socrates has said, gentlemen.
187C But whether you are willing to be questioned about such matters and to give account of them, you must decide for yourselves, Nicias and Laches. As far as Melesias here and I are concerned, we would certainly be pleased if the two of you were willing to give complete answers to all of Socrates' questions. Because, as I started to say right at the beginning, the reason we invited you to advise us on these matters was that we supposed that you would naturally have given some thought to such things—especially so since your sons, like ours, are very
D   nearly of an age to be-educated. So, if you have no objection, speak up and look into the subject along with Socrates, exchanging arguments with each other. Because he is right in saying that it is about the most important of our affairs that we are consulting. So decide if you think this is what ought to be done.

NICIAS   It is quite clear to me, Lysimachus, that your knowledge of Socrates is limited to your acquaintance with his father and that you have had no contact with the man himself, except when he was a child—I suppose he may have min-
E   gled with you and your fellow demesmen, following along with his father at the temple or at some other public gathering. But you are obviously still unacquainted with the man as he is now he has grown up.

LYSIMACHUS   What exactly do you mean, Nicias?

NICIAS   You don't appear to me to know that whoever comes into close contact with Socrates and associates with him

---

22. The same proverb appears at *Gorgias* 514E. A wine jar is the largest pot; one ought to learn pottery on something smaller.

in conversation must necessarily, even if he began by conversing about something quite different in the first place, keep on being led about by the man's arguments until he submits to answering questions about himself concerning both his present manner of life and the life he has lived hitherto. And when 188A he does submit to this questioning, you don't realize that Socrates will not let him go before he has well and truly tested every last detail.[23] I personally am accustomed to the man and know that one has to put up with this kind of treatment from him, and further, I know perfectly well that I myself will have to submit to it. I take pleasure in the man's company, Lysimachus, and don't regard it as at all a bad thing to have it brought to our attention that we have done or are doing B wrong. Rather I think that a man who does not run away from such treatment but is willing, according to the saying of Solon, to value learning as long as he lives,[24] not supposing that old age brings him wisdom of itself, will necessarily pay more attention to the rest of his life. For me there is nothing unusual or unpleasant in being examined by Socrates, but I realized some time ago that the conversation would not be C about the boys but about ourselves, if Socrates were present.[25] As I say, I don't myself mind talking with Socrates in whatever way he likes—but find out how Laches here feels about such things.

LACHES I have just one feeling about discussions, Nicias, or, if you like, not one but two, because to some I might seem to be a discussion-lover and to others a discussion-hater.[26] Whenever I hear a man discussing virtue or some kind of

23. Nicias has given an excellent description of Socratic method. Cf. *Apology* 29Dff.

24. Solon is the Athenian poet and lawgiver of the early sixth century. He was traditionally an ancestor of Plato's on the maternal side. The line referred to is *gēraskō d' aiei polla didaskomenos* ("I grow old ever learning many things.") See below 189A and *Republic* 536CD.

25. But see above 185C and note.

26. For *misologia* or hatred of argument see *Phaedo* 89Cff. and *Republic* 411D.

wisdom, then, if he really is a man and worthy of the words
188D   he utters, I am completely delighted to see the appropriateness
and harmony existing between the speaker and his words.[27]
And such a man seems to me to be genuinely musical, producing the most beautiful harmony, not on the lyre or some
other pleasurable instrument, but actually rendering his own
life harmonious by fitting his deeds to his words in a truly
Dorian mode, not in the Ionian, nor even, I think, in the
Phrygian or Lydian, but in the only harmony that is genuinely Greek.[28] The discourse of such a man gladdens my heart
E   and makes everyone think that I am a discussion-lover because
of the enthusiastic way in which I welcome what is said; but
the man who acts in the opposite way distresses me, and the
better he speaks, the worse I feel, so that his discourse makes
me look like a discussion-hater. Now I have no acquaintance
with the words of Socrates, but before now, I believe, I have
had experience of his deeds, and there I found him a person
privileged to speak fair words and to indulge in every kind of
189A   frankness. So if he possesses this ability too, I am in sympathy
with the man, and I would submit to being examined by such
a person with the greatest pleasure, nor would I find learning
burdensome, because I too agree with Solon, though with one
reservation—I wish to grow old learning many things,[29] but
from good men only. Let Solon grant me this point, that the
teacher should himself be good, so that I may not show myself
a stupid pupil taking no delight in learning. Whether my

27. The familiar Greek contrast between word and deed (*logos* and
ergon) is a dominant theme of the dialogue, as has been pointed out by
Michael J. O'Brien, "The Unity of the *Laches,*" *Yale Classical Studies*
XVIII (1963) : 133-147. (See also Robert J. Hoerber, "Plato's *Laches,*"
Classical Philology LXIII (1968) : 95-105) . To think of Laches as all action
and Nicias as all thought would be incorrect, however. See Introduction
pp. 6-8.

28. The Greeks believed that the various musical modes were productive of various distinct states of character. See *Republic* 398Dff. and
Aristotle *Politics* 1290a22ff., 1340a40ff., and 1342a33ff. Aristotle speaks at
1342b12 of the particularly steady and manly character of the Dorian
mode.

29. See above 188B.

teacher is to be younger than I am or not yet famous or has any other such peculiarity troubles me not at all. To you then, 189B Socrates, I present myself as someone for you to teach and to refute in whatever manner you please, and, on the other hand, you are welcome to any knowledge I have myself. Because this has been my opinion of your character since that day on which we shared a common danger and you gave me a sample of your valor—the sort a man must give if he is to render a good account of himself. So say whatever you like and don't let the difference in our ages concern you at all.[30]

SOCRATES   We certainly can't find fault with you for not   C being ready both to give advice and to join in the common search.

LYSIMACHUS   But the task is clearly ours, Socrates (for I count you as one of ourselves), so take my place and find out on behalf of the young men what we need to learn from these people, and then, by talking to the boys, join us in giving them advice. Because, on account of my age, I very often forget what questions I was going to ask, and I forget the answers as well. Then, if fresh arguments start up in the middle, my memory is not exactly good. So you do the talking and exam-   D ine among yourselves the topics we proposed. And I will listen, and when I have heard your conversation, I will do whatever you people think best and so will Melesias here.

SOCRATES   Let us do what Lysimachus and Melesias suggest, Nicias and Laches. Perhaps it won't be a bad idea to ask ourselves the sort of question which we proposed to investigate just now: what teachers have we had in this sort of instruction, and what other persons have we made better? However, I think   E there is another sort of inquiry that will bring us to the same point and is perhaps one that begins somewhat more nearly from the beginning. Suppose we know, about anything whatsoever, that if it is added to another thing, it makes that thing

---

30. Socrates is younger than any of the other four adults (181D), but the difference between him and the two generals cannot be very great.

better, and furthermore, we are able to make the addition, then clearly we know the very thing about which we should be consulting as to how one might obtain it most easily and best. Perhaps you don't understand what I mean, but will do

190A so more easily this way: suppose we know that sight, when added to the eyes, makes better those eyes to which it is added, and furthermore, we are able to add it to the eyes, then clearly we know what this very thing sight is, about which we should be consulting as to how one might obtain it most easily and best. Because if we didn't know what sight in itself was, nor hearing, we would hardly be worthy counsellors and doctors about either the eyes or the ears as to the manner in which

B either sight or hearing might best be obtained.[31]

LACHES   You are right, Socrates.

SOCRATES   Well then, Laches, aren't these two now asking our advice as to the manner in which virtue might be added to the souls of their sons to make them better?

LACHES   Yes, indeed.

SOCRATES   Then isn't it necessary for us to start out knowing what virtue is? Because if we are not absolutely cer-

C tain what it is, how are we going to advise anyone as to the best method of obtaining it?[32]

LACHES   I do not think that there is any way in which we can do this, Socrates.

SOCRATES   We say then, Laches, that we know what it is.

LACHES   Yes, we do say so.

SOCRATES   And what we know, we must, I suppose, be able to state?[33]

LACHES   Of course.

SOCRATES   Let us not, O best of men, begin straight-away with an investigation of the whole of virtue—that would

31. The procedure here is the reverse of 185C, where we had illustrations first, general principle afterwards.

32. This amounts to the position taken at the beginning of the *Meno* 70Aff. Cf. *Protagoras* 360Eff.

33. A similar point is made at *Charmides* 158Eff.

perhaps be too great a task—but let us first see if we have a sufficient knowledge of a part.[34] Then it is likely that the inves-   **190D** tigation will be easier for us.

LACHES   Yes, let's do it the way you want, Socrates.

SOCRATES   Well, which one of the parts of virtue should we choose? Or isn't it obvious that we ought to take the one to which the technique of fighting in armor appears to lead? I suppose everyone would think it leads to courage, wouldn't they?[35]

LACHES   I think they certainly would.

SOCRATES   Then let us undertake first of all, Laches, to state what courage is. Then after this we will go on to inves-   **E** tigate in what way it could be added to the young, to the extent that the addition can be made through occupations and studies.[36] But try to state what I ask, namely, what courage is.

LACHES   Good heavens, Socrates, there is no difficulty about that: if a man is willing to remain at his post and to defend himself against the enemy without running away, then you may rest assured that he is a man of courage.[37]

---

34. This is a crucial move. By 199C the discussion of courage has led to the suggestion (one which I think Plato means to retain) that this single virtue may be "the knowledge of practically all goods and evils put together." The discussion of temperance in the *Charmides* leads to the same conclusion, so that the two dialogues together show Plato's way of demonstrating the unity of the virtues. (Cf. also *Protagoras* 329C-334A and 349A-362A.)

35. We may suppose, also, that Plato chooses courage because it is the virtue of which we might expect a definition from a general. Cf. the questioning of the temperate Charmides as to the nature of temperance (*Charmides* 156D, 158E) and of the self-designated expert on religious matters, Euthyphro, as to the nature of holiness or piety (*Euthyphro* 4E, 5D). So, too, the young friends Lysis and Menexenus are invited to state what a friend is (*Lysis* 211Eff.)

36. Since a satisfactory definition of courage is never reached, we do not have a discussion of this second topic.

37. At a point more than half-way through the dialogue we finally reach the first definition. Like Meno, when asked to define virtue (*Meno* 71E), Laches sees no difficulty in Socrates' question. Note, incidentally, that Laches defines, not courage, but a courageous man. The man and his virtues (or vices) are very largely interchangeable for Plato.

SOCRATES   Well spoken, Laches. But perhaps I am to blame for not making myself clear; the result is that you did not answer the question I had in mind but a different one.[38]

LACHES   What do you mean, Socrates?

191A   SOCRATES   I will tell you if I can. That man, I suppose, is courageous whom you yourself mention, that is, the man who fights the enemy while remaining at his post?

LACHES   Yes, that is my view.

SOCRATES   And I agree. But what about this man, the one who fights with the enemy, not holding his ground, but in retreat?

LACHES   What did you mean, in retreat?

SOCRATES   Why, I mean the way the Scythians are said to fight, as much retreating as pursuing; and then I imagine that Homer is praising the horses of Aeneas when he says they

B   know how "to pursue and fly quickly this way and that", and he praises Aeneas himself for his knowledge of fear and he calls him "counsellor of fright."[39]

LACHES   And Homer is right, Socrates, because he was speaking of chariots, and it was the Scythian horsemen to which you referred. Now cavalry do fight in this fashion, but the hoplites in the manner I describe.

SOCRATES   Except perhaps the Spartan hoplites, Laches.

C   Because they say that at Plataea the Spartans, when they were up against the soldiers carrying wicker shields, were not willing to stand their ground and fight against them but ran away. Then when the ranks of the Persians were broken, they turned and fought, just like cavalrymen, and so won that particular battle.[40]

LACHES   You are right.

---

38. Laches' definition is too narrow: see below 191C.

39. *Iliad* V, 222-3 and VIII, 106-108. Plato distorts the meaning to suit his own purposes.

40. The battle of Plataea (in Boeotia) was fought at the end of August 479. The Greeks under Pausanias defeated the Persians under Mardonius. Plato's description of the battle is not consistent with the one in Herodotus IX 61-63.

SOCRATES   So as I said just now, my poor questioning
is to blame for your poor answer, because I wanted to learn
from you not only what constitutes courage for a hoplite but   191D
for a horseman as well and for every sort of warrior. And I
wanted to include not only those who are courageous in warfare but also those who are brave in dangers at sea, and the
ones who show courage in illness and poverty and affairs of
state; and then again I wanted to include not only those who
are brave in the face of pain and fear but also those who are
clever at fighting desire and pleasure, whether by standing   E
their ground or running away—because there are some men,
aren't there, Laches, who are brave in matters like these?[41]

LACHES   Very much so, Socrates.

SOCRATES   So all these men are brave, but some possess
courage in pleasures, some in pains, some in desires, and some
in fears. And others, I think, show cowardice in the same
respects.

LACHES   Yes, they do.

SOCRATES   Then what are courage and cowardice? This
is what I wanted to find out. So try again to state first what is
the courage that is the same in all these cases.[42] Or don't you
yet have a clear understanding of what I mean?

LACHES   Not exactly.

SOCRATES   Well, I mean something like this: suppose   192A
I asked what speed was, which we find in running and in playing the lyre and in speaking and in learning and in many other
instances—in fact we may say we display the quality, so far as
it is worth mentioning, in movements of the arms or legs or
tongue or voice or thought? Or isn't this the way you too
would express it?

LACHES   Yes, indeed.

SOCRATES   Then if anyone should ask me, "Socrates,
what do you say it is which you call swiftness in all these

41. Cf. *Republic* 429Cff. and *Laws* 633CD. Aristotle (*Nicomachean
Ethics* III, 6, 1115a6-24) thinks these other sorts of courage are only
called such by analogy.
42. Cf. *Euthyphro* 5D and *Meno* 72C.

192B   cases," I would answer him that what I call swiftness is the power of accomplishing a great deal in a short time, whether in speech or in running or all the other cases.[43]

     LACHES   And you would be right.

     SOCRATES   Then make an effort yourself, Laches, to speak in the same way about courage. What faculty is it which, because it is the same in pleasure and in pain and in all the other cases in which we were just saying it occurred, is therefore called courage?

     LACHES   Well then, I think it is a sort of endurance of
C   the soul, if it is necessary to say what its nature is in all these cases.[44]

     SOCRATES   But it is necessary, at any rate if we are to give an answer to our question. Now this is what appears to me: I think that you don't regard every kind of endurance as courage. The reason I think so is this: I am fairly sure, Laches, that you regard courage as a very fine thing.[45]

     LACHES   One of the finest, you may be sure.

     SOCRATES   And you would say that endurance accompanied by wisdom is a fine and noble thing?[46]

     LACHES   Very much so.

D   SOCRATES   Suppose it is accompanied by folly? Isn't it just the opposite, harmful and injurious?

     LACHES   Yes.

---

43. Although Plato does not provide us with conclusive definitions of moral terms, he does on occasion allow Socrates to give precise definitions of other sorts of terms. See *Meno* 75B and 76A (figure), *Theaetetus* 147C (clay), and 208D (the sun.)

44. Laches' second definition, although meeting Socrates' requirements better than the first (190E), will prove to be too broad instead of too narrow. According to O'Brien (see on 188D), this notion of endurance or steadfastness is never given up, however. (See his article p. 140, and see below 194A.)

45. Cf. the similar step at *Charmides* 159C.

46. Here is the first appearance, in this dialogue, of the Socratic view that virtue is knowledge (or wisdom). Plato's purpose in the next few pages is to show that our admiration of foolish endurance is really an admiration of foolhardiness, not of courage. With this passage should be compared *Protagoras* 349E-350C, and 359B-360E.

SOCRATES   And you are going to call a thing fine which is of the injurious and harmful sort?

LACHES   No, that wouldn't be right, Socrates.

SOCRATES   Then you won't allow this kind of endurance to be courage, since it is not fine, whereas courage *is* fine.

LACHES   You are right.

SOCRATES   Then, according to your view, it would be wise endurance which would be courage.

LACHES   So it seems.

SOCRATES   Let us see then in what respect it is wise—is   192E
it so with respect to everything both great and small? For instance, if a man were to show endurance in spending his money wisely, knowing that by spending it he would get more, would you call this man courageous?

LACHES   Heavens no, not I.

SOCRATES   Well, suppose a man is a doctor, and his son or some other patient is ill with inflammation of the lungs and begs him for something to eat or drink, and the man doesn't give in but perseveres in refusing?[47]   193A

LACHES   No, this would certainly not be courage either, not at all.

SOCRATES   Well, suppose a man endures in battle, and his willingness to fight is based on wise calculation because he knows that others are coming to his aid and that he will be fighting men who are fewer than those on his side, and inferior to them, and in addition his position is stronger: would you say that this man, with his kind of wisdom and preparation, endures more courageously or a man in the opposite camp who is willing to remain and hold out?

LACHES   The one in the opposite camp, Socrates, I   B
should say.

SOCRATES   But surely the endurance of this man is more foolish than that of the other.

LACHES   You are right.

---

47. Socrates' example would, however, appear to fall into the group of cases mentioned at 191E.

SOCRATES   And you would say that the man who shows endurance in a cavalry attack and has knowledge of horsemanship is less courageous than the man who lacks this knowledge.

LACHES   Yes, I would.

SOCRATES   And the one who endures with knowledge of slinging or archery or some other art is the less courageous.

193C   LACHES   Yes indeed.

SOCRATES   And as many as would be willing to endure in diving down into wells[48] without being skilled, or to endure in any other similar situation, you say are braver than those who are skilled in these things.

LACHES   Why, what else would anyone say, Socrates?

SOCRATES   Nothing, if that is what he thought.

LACHES   Well, this is what I think at any rate.

SOCRATES   And certainly, Laches, such people run risks and endure more foolishly than those who do a thing with art.

LACHES   They clearly do.

D   SOCRATES   Now foolish daring and endurance was found by us to be not only disgraceful but harmful, in what we said earlier.

LACHES   Quite so.

SOCRATES   But courage was agreed to be a noble thing.

LACHES   Yes, it was.

SOCRATES   But now, on the contrary, we are saying that a disgraceful thing, foolish endurance, is courage.

LACHES   Yes, we seem to be.

SOCRATES   And do you think we are talking sense?

LACHES   Heavens no, Socrates, I certainly don't.

SOCRATES   Then I don't suppose, Laches, that according
E   to your statement you and I are tuned to the Dorian mode,

---

48. Professor W. B. Stanford writes me that Plato may be referring here to people who were willing to dive down into the water of wells or cisterns to recover vessels dropped by water-drawers. Their "diving" was not a matter of plunging in from the top of a well, but of descending into the water after they had climbed down or been lowered down on a rope. Cf. *Protagoras* 350A. Hesychius' *Lexicon* defines divers as "those who send up jars from wells." (Conceivably the jars could be full. See *LSJ* s.v. *kolumbētēs*.)

because our deeds are not harmonizing with our words.[49] In deeds I think anyone would say that we partook of courage, but in words I don't suppose he would, if he were to listen to our present discussion.

LACHES   You are absolutely right.

SOCRATES   Well then: is it good for us to be in such a state?

LACHES   Certainly not, in no way whatsoever.

SOCRATES   But are you willing that we should agree with our statement to a certain extent?

LACHES   To what extent and with what statement?

SOCRATES   With the one that commands us to endure. **194A** If you are willing, let us hold our ground in the search and let us endure, so that courage itself won't make fun of us for not searching for it courageously—if endurance should perhaps be courage after all.

LACHES   I am ready not to give up, Socrates, although I am not really accustomed to arguments of this kind. But an absolute desire for victory has seized me with respect to our conversation, and I am really getting annoyed at being un- **B** able to express what I think in this fashion.[50] I still think I know what courage is, but I can't understand how it has escaped me just now so that I can't pin it down in words and say what it is.

SOCRATES   Well, my friend, a good hunter ought to pursue the trail and not give up.

LACHES   Absolutely.

SOCRATES   Then, if you agree, let's also summon Nicias here to the hunt—he might get on much better.[51]

LACHES   I am willing—why not? **C**

---

49. See above, 188D.
50. This feeling on the part of Laches is a necessary stage in the Socratic *elenchus*. Cf. *Meno* 79Eff. and *Theaetetus* 168B. See Introduction, p. 7.
51. The metaphor of the hunt is a favorite one with Plato. Cf. *Lysis* 218C, *Euthydemus* 291B, *Parmenides* 128B, and, especially, *Republic* 432Bff.

SOCRATES   Come along then, Nicias, and, if you can, res-
cue your friends who are storm-tossed by the argument and
find themselves in trouble. You see, of course, that our affairs
are in a bad way, so state what you think courage is and get
us out of our difficulties as well as confirming your own view
by putting it into words.

NICIAS   I have been thinking for some time that you are
not defining courage in the right way, Socrates. And you are
not employing the excellent observation I have heard you
make before now.[52]

SOCRATES   What one was that, Nicias?

194D   NICIAS   I have often heard you say that every one of us
is good with respect to that in which he is wise and bad in
respect to that in which he is ignorant.

SOCRATES   By heaven, you are right, Nicias.

NICIAS   Therefore, if a man is really courageous, it is
clear that he is wise.

SOCRATES   You hear that, Laches?

LACHES   I do, but I don't understand exactly what he
means.

SOCRATES   Well, I think I understand him, and the
man seems to me to be saying that courage is some kind of
wisdom.

LACHES   Why, what sort of wisdom is he talking about,
Socrates?

E   SOCRATES   Why don't you ask him?

LACHES   All right.

SOCRATES   Come, Nicias, tell him what sort of wisdom
courage would be according to your view. I don't suppose it
is skill in flute playing.[53]

---

52. Cf. *Republic* 349E. Unlike Laches, Nicias has conversed with Socrates before. Cf. 187Eff. and 188E.

53. The suggestion that courage is wisdom (or knowledge) immediately raises the question of subject matter. That is, if knowledge is what
I have called a *tinos*-word (see Preface pp. viii–ix), to say that a thing
is knowledge is to say that it is knowledge of something. Of flute playing?
Of lyre playing? These are first-order *technai;* Nicias' answer (195A) is
puzzling to Laches because it seems to refer to a *techne* of a higher level.

NICIAS   Of course not.

SOCRATES   And not in lyre playing either.

NICIAS   Far from it.

SOCRATES   But what is this knowledge and of what?

LACHES   You are questioning him in just the right way.

SOCRATES   Let him state what kind of knowledge it is.

NICIAS   What I say, Laches, is that it is the knowledge of the fearful and the hopeful in war and in every other situation.[54]   195A

LACHES   How strangely he talks, Socrates.

SOCRATES   What do you have in mind when you say this, Laches?

LACHES   What do I have in mind? Why, I take wisdom to be quite a different thing from courage.

SOCRATES   Well, Nicias, at any rate, says it isn't.

LACHES   He certainly does—that's the nonsense he talks.

SOCRATES   Well, let's instruct him instead of making fun of him.

NICIAS   Very well, but it strikes me, Socrates, that Laches wants to prove that I am talking nonsense simply because he was shown to be that sort of person himself a moment ago.   B

LACHES   Quite so, Nicias, and I shall try to demonstrate that very thing, because you *are* talking nonsense.[55] Take an immediate example: in cases of illness, aren't the doctors the ones who know what is to be feared? Or do you think the courageous are the people who know? Perhaps you call the doctors the courageous?

NICIAS   No, of course not.

LACHES   And I don't imagine you mean the farmers either, even though I do suppose they are the ones who know what is to be feared in farming. And all the other craftsmen

54. This is the third definition (Nicias' first). Cf. *Protagoras* 360CD.

55. It should be noted that Laches now becomes the questioner and that his questions serve to drive home the distinction already suggested at 194E between first- and second-order *technai*. Then at 195C Nicias takes the lead until 196A. It is not until 196C that Socrates takes the discussion into his own hands once more.

know what is to be feared and hoped for in their particular

195C   arts. But these people are in no way courageous all the same.

SOCRATES   What does Laches mean, Nicias? Because he does seems to be saying something.

NICIAS   Yes, he is saying something, but what he says is not true.

SOCRATES   How so?

NICIAS   He thinks a doctor's knowledge of the sick amounts to something more than being able to describe health and disease, whereas I think their knowledge is restricted to just this. Do you suppose, Laches, that when a man's recovery is more to be feared than his illness, the doctors know this? Or don't you think there are many cases in which it would be better not to get up from an illness? Tell me this: do you

D   maintain that in all cases to live is preferable? In many cases, is it not better to die?[56]

LACHES   Well, I agree with you on this point at least.

NICIAS   And do you suppose that the same things are to be feared by those for whom it is an advantage to die as by those for whom it is an advantage to live?

LACHES   No, I don't.

NICIAS   But do you grant this knowledge to the doctors or to any other craftsmen except the one who knows what is and what is not to be feared, who is the one I call courageous?

SOCRATES   Do you understand what he is saying, Laches?

E   LACHES   Yes I do—he is calling the seers the courageous.[57] Because who else will know for whom it is better to live than to die? What about you, Nicias—do you admit to being a seer, or, if you are not a seer, to not being courageous?

56. Nicias is working towards the point that courage is really a knowledge of good and evil. Cf. the pilot of *Gorgias* 511Dff., who does not presume to say whether he has benefited his passengers by saving them from being drowned.

57. Plato's readers could not fail to be reminded here that Nicias' superstitious reliance on seers was a major factor in the failure of the Athenian expedition to Sicily. For a lively account of the whole campaign, see Peter Green, *Armada from Athens* (London, 1970). Aristophanes in his *Birds* 640 coined a special verb, *mellonikian*, meaning to delay victory in the manner of Nicias, or as Green translates it (p. 180), to "Niciashuffle".

NICIAS Well, what of it? Don't you, for your part, think it is appropriate for a seer to know what is to be feared and what is to be hoped?

LACHES Yes, I do, because I don't see for what other person it would be.

NICIAS Much more for the man I am talking about, my friend, because the seer needs to know only the signs of what is to be, whether a man will experience death or illness or loss of property, or will experience victory or defeat, in battle or   196A
in any other sort of contest. But why is it more suitable for the seer than for anyone else to judge for whom it is better to suffer or not to suffer these things?

LACHES It isn't clear to me from this, Socrates, what he is trying to say. Because he doesn't select either the seer or the doctor or anyone else as the man he calls courageous, unless some god is the person he means.[58] Nicias appears to me unwilling to make a gentlemanly admission that he is talking   B
nonsense, but he twists this way and that in an attempt to cover up his difficulty. Even you and I could have executed a similar twist just now if we had wanted to avoid the appearance of contradicting ourselves. If we were making speeches in a court of law, there might be some point in doing this, but as things are, why should anyone adorn himself senselessly with empty words in a gathering like this?

SOCRATES I see no reason why he should, Laches. But let   C
us see if Nicias thinks he is saying something and is not just talking for the sake of talking. Let us find out from him more clearly what it is he means, and if he is really saying something, we will agree with him, but if not, we will instruct him.

LACHES You go ahead and question him, Socrates, if you want to find out. I think perhaps I have asked enough.

SOCRATES I have no objection, since the inquiry will be a joint effort on behalf of us both.

LACHES Very well.

---

58. Laches is on the right track, since the man who has the sort of second-order knowledge Nicias means will have to have a kind of god-like omniscience. Cf. *Charmides* 174A and see below 199Cff.

SOCRATES   Then tell me, Nicias, or rather tell *us*, be-
196D   cause Laches and I are sharing the argument: you say that
courage is knowledge of the grounds of fear and hope?

NICIAS   Yes, I do.

SOCRATES   Then this knowledge is something possessed
by very few indeed if, as you say, neither the doctor nor the
seer will have it and won't be courageous without acquiring
this particular knowledge.[59] Isn't that what you're saying?

NICIAS   Just so.

SOCRATES   Then, as the proverb says, it is true that this
is not something "every sow would know,"[60] and she would
not be courageous?

NICIAS   I don't think so.

E   SOCRATES   Then it is obvious, Nicias, that you do not
regard the Crommyon sow[61] as having been courageous. I
say this not as a joke, but because I think that anyone taking
this position must necessarily deny courage to any wild beast
or else admit that some wild beast, a lion or a leopard or
some sort of wild boar, is wise enough to know what is so difficult that very few men understand it. And, similarly, the man
who defines courage as you define it would have to assert that
a lion and a stag, a bull and a monkey are all naturally
courageous.

197A   LACHES   By heaven, you talk well, Socrates. Give us an
honest answer to this, Nicias—whether you say that these wild
beasts, whom we all admit to be courageous, are wiser than we
in these respects, or whether you dare to oppose the general
view and say that they are not courageous.

NICIAS   By no means, Laches, do I call courageous wild
beasts or anything else that, for lack of understanding, does

59. That is, to have a first-order *techne* will not guarantee having one
of the second order.

60. To the Greek, the pig usually connotes stupidity rather than dirti-
ness or greed. (Cf. *Theaetetus* 161C.) Socrates probably introduces the
proverb just here because he wants to talk about animals. (According to
the Scholiast, the actual proverb was "even a dog or a pig would know.")

61. The famous sow of Crommyon (near Corinth) was killed by Theseus. See Plutarch *Theseus* 9.

not fear what should be feared. Rather, I would call them rash and mad.[62] Or do you really suppose I call all children courageous, who fear nothing because they have no sense? On the contrary, I think that rashness and courage are not the same thing. My view is that very few have a share of courage and foresight,[63] but that a great many, men and women and children and wild animals, partake in boldness and audacity and rashness and lack of foresight. These cases, which you and the man in the street call courageous, I call rash, whereas the courageous ones are the sensible people I was talking about.

197B

C

LACHES You see, Socrates, how the man decks himself out in words and does it well in his own opinion. Those whom everyone agrees to be courageous he attempts to deprive of that distinction.

NICIAS I'm not depriving you of it, Laches, so cheer up. I declare that you are wise, and Lamachus[64] too, so long as you are courageous, and I say the same of a great many other Athenians.

LACHES I shan't say anything about that—though I could—in case you should call me a typical Aexonian.[65]

SOCRATES Never mind him, Laches. I don't think you realize that he has procured this wisdom from our friend Damon, and Damon spends most of his time with Prodicus,[66]

D

---

62. Nicias has come up with the point Socrates is after, that rashness should be separated off from courage. This was really the point at issue in the rejection of foolish endurance at 192Cff.

63. Cf. *Laws* 963E, on children and animals.

64. Lamachus shared the command of the Sicilian expedition with Nicias and Alcibiades; he died at Syracuse. See Thucydides VI, 8, 49, 101. He makes an appearance in Aristophanes' *Acharnians* 566ff.

65. According to the Scholiast, the people of the deme Aexone were regarded as abusive speakers. Hence there was even a verb *aixōneuesthai*, to speak (slanderously) like an Aexonian.

66. The sophist Prodicus usually appears in Plato as a proponent of nice distinctions in words. (Cf. *Charmides* 163D.) For a speech of his on this topic, see *Protagoras* 337Aff., and see also 358D where he distinguishes between fear and terror. Prodicus was the author of a speech "The Choice of Heracles", which may be found in Xenophon's *Memorabilia* II, 1, 21-34. For Damon, see above 180D.

who has the reputation of being best among the sophists at
making such verbal distinctions.

LACHES   Well, Socrates, it is certainly more fitting for
a sophist to make such clever distinctions than for a man the
city thinks worthy to be its leader.

97E   SOCRATES   Well, I suppose it would be fitting, my good
friend, for the man in charge of the greatest affairs to have the
greatest share of wisdom. But I think it worthwhile to ask
Nicias what he has in mind when he defines courage in this
way.

LACHES   Well then, you ask him, Socrates.

SOCRATES   This is just what I intend to do, my good
friend. But don't therefore suppose that I shall let you out of
your share of the argument. Pay attention and join me in examining what is being said.

LACHES   Very well, if that seems necessary.

SOCRATES   Yes, it does. And you, Nicias, tell us again
198A   from the beginning—you know that when we were investigating
courage at the beginning of the argument, we were investigating it as a part of virtue?[67]

NICIAS   Yes, we were.

SOCRATES   And didn't you give your answer supposing
that it was a part, and, as such, one among a number of other
parts, all of which taken together were called virtue?

NICIAS   Yes, why not?

SOCRATES   And do you also speak of the same parts
that I do? In addition to courage, I call temperance and justice and everything else of this kind parts of virtue. Don't
you?[68]

B   NICIAS   Yes, indeed.

SOCRATES   Stop there. We are in agreement on these
points, but let us investigate the grounds of fear and confidence to make sure that you don't regard them in one way

---

67. At 190C.
68. Cf. *Protagoras* 329C and *Meno* 88A. The so-called "cardinal" virtues (justice, wisdom, courage, and temperance) are a special feature of
the *Republic*. (See 428Aff.)

and we in another. We will tell you what we think about them, and if you do not agree, you shall instruct us. We regard as fearful things those that produce fear, and as hopeful things those that do not produce fear; and fear is produced not by evils which have happened or are happening but by those which are anticipated. Because fear is the expectation of a future evil[69]—or isn't this your opinion too, Laches?

LACHES   Very much so, Socrates. 198C

SOCRATES   You hear what we have to say, Nicias: that fearful things are future evils, and the ones inspiring hope are either future non-evils or future goods.[70] Do you agree with this or have you some other view on the subject?

NICIAS   I agree with this one.

SOCRATES   And you declare that knowledge of just these things is courage?

NICIAS   Exactly so.

SOCRATES   Let us find out if we all agree on still a third point.

NICIAS   What one is that?

SOCRATES   I will explain. It seems to me and my friend D here that of the various things with which knowledge is concerned, there is not one kind of knowledge by which we know how things have happened in the past, and another by which we know how they are happening at the present time, and still another by which we know how what has not yet happened might best come to be in the future, but that the knowledge is the same in each case.[71] For instance, in the case of health, there is no other art related to the past, the present, and the future except that of medicine, which, although it is a single art, surveys what is, what was, and what is likely to be in the future. Again, in the case of the fruits of the earth, E the art of farming conforms to the same pattern. And I suppose that both of you could bear witness that, in the case of

---

69. Substantially the same definition is suggested at *Protagoras* 358D.

70. It is interesting that the neutral cases are cases of hope.

71. Each science is a whole, in other words, and its truths are true at all times.

the affairs of war, the art of generalship is that which best foresees the future and the other times—nor does this art consider it necessary to be ruled by the art of the seer, but to rule **199A** *it,* as being better acquainted with both present and future in the affairs of war. In fact, the law decrees, not that the seer should command the general, but that the general should command the seer.[72] Is this what we shall say, Laches?

LACHES   Yes, it is.

SOCRATES   Well then, do you agree with us, Nicias, that the same knowledge has understanding of the same things, whether future, present, or past?

NICIAS   Yes, that is how it seems to me, Socrates.

SOCRATES   Now, my good friend, you say that courage is **B** the knowledge of the fearful and the hopeful, isn't that so?

NICIAS   Yes, it is.

SOCRATES   And it was agreed that fearful and hopeful things were future goods and future evils.

NICIAS   Yes, it was.

SOCRATES   And that the same knowledge is of the same things—future ones and all other kinds.

NICIAS   Yes, that is the case.

SOCRATES   Then courage is not knowledge of the fearful and the hopeful only, because it understands not simply future **C** goods and evils, but those of the present and the past and all times, just as is the case with the other kinds of knowledge.

NICIAS   So it seems, at any rate.

SOCRATES   Then you have told us about what amounts to a third part of courage, Nicias, whereas we asked you what the whole of courage was. And now it appears, according to your view, that courage is the knowledge not just of the fearful and the hopeful, but in your own opinion, it would be the **D** knowledge of practically all goods and evils put together. Do you agree to this new change, Nicias, or what do you say?

NICIAS   That seems right to me, Socrates.

---

72. Another reference to the ultimate fate of Nicias: see above 195E. For Plato's opinion of seers, see *Meno* 99C and *Statesman* 290Cff.

SOCRATES   Then does a man with this kind of knowledge seem to depart from virtue in any respect if he really knows, in the case of all goods whatsoever, what they are and will be and have been, and similarly in the case of evils? And do you regard that man as lacking in temperance or justice and holiness to whom alone belongs the ability to deal circumspectly with both gods and men with respect to both the fearful and its opposite, and to provide himself with good things through his knowledge of how to associate with them correctly?   199E

NICIAS   I think you have a point, Socrates.

SOCRATES   Then the thing you are now talking about, Nicias, would not be a part of virtue but rather virtue entire.

NICIAS   So it seems.

SOCRATES   And we have certainly stated that courage is one of the parts of virtue.

NICIAS   Yes, we have.

SOCRATES   Then what we are saying now does not appear to hold good.

NICIAS   Apparently not.

SOCRATES   Then we have not discovered, Nicias, what courage is.[73]

NICIAS   We don't appear to.

LACHES   But I, my dear Nicias, felt sure you would make the discovery after you were so scornful of me while I was answering Socrates. In fact, I had great hopes that with the help of Damon's wisdom you would solve the whole problem.   200A

NICIAS   That's a fine attitude of yours, Laches, to think it no longer to be of any importance that you yourself were just now shown to be a person who knows nothing about courage. What interests you is whether I will turn out to be a person of the same kind. Apparently it will make no difference to you to be ignorant of those things which a man of any pretensions ought to know, so long as you include me in

---

73. This is the usual outcome of the early dialogues. We have, however, found out more than Socrates' remark would indicate.

200B your ignorance. Well, you seem to me to be acting in a thoroughly human fashion by noticing everybody except yourself. As far as I am concerned I think enough has been said on the topic for the present, and if any point has not been covered sufficiently, then later on I think we can correct it both with the help of Damon—whom you think it right to laugh at, though you have never seen the man—and with that of others. And when I feel secure on these points, I will instruct you too

C and won't begrudge the effort—because you seem to me to be sadly in need of learning.

LACHES You are a clever man, Nicias, I know. All the same, I advise Lysimachus here and Melesias to say good-bye to you and me as teachers of the young men and to retain the services of this man Socrates, as I said in the beginning. If my boys were the same age, this is what I would do.

NICIAS And I agree: if Socrates is really willing to undertake the supervision of the boys, then don't look for anyone

D else. In fact I would gladly entrust Niceratus[74] to him, if he is willing. But whenever I bring up the subject in any way, he always recommends other people to me but is unwilling to take on the job himself. But see if Socrates might be more willing to listen to you, Lysimachus.

LYSIMACHUS Well, he should, Nicias, since I myself would be willing to do a great many things for him which I would not be willing to do for practically anyone else. What do you say, Socrates? Will you comply with our request and take an active part with us in helping the young men to become as good as possible?

E SOCRATES Well, it would be a terrible thing, Lysimachus, to be unwilling to join in assisting any man to become as good as possible. If in the conversations we have just had I had seemed to be knowing and the other two had not, then it would be right to issue a special invitation to me to perform this task; but as the matter stands, we were all in the same difficulty. Why then should anybody choose one of us in preference

74. See above, on 179B.

to another? What I think is that he ought to choose none of us. 201A
But as things are, see whether the suggestion I am about to
make may not be a good one: what I say we ought to do, my
friends—since this is just between ourselves—is to join in
searching for the best possible teacher, first for ourselves—we
really need one—and then for the young men, sparing neither
money nor anything else. What I don't advise is that we remain
as we are. And if anyone laughs at us because we think it
worthwhile to spend our time in school at our age, then I think B
we should confront him with the saying of Homer, "Modesty
is not a good mate for a needy man."[75] And, not paying any
attention to what anyone may say, let us join together in looking after both our own interests and those of the boys.

    LYSIMACHUS   I like what you say, Socrates, and the fact
that I am the oldest makes me the most eager to go to school
along with the boys. Just do this for me: come to my house
early tomorrow—don't refuse—so that we may make plans C
about these matters, but let us make an end of our present
conversation.

    SOCRATES   I shall do what you say, Lysimachus, and
come to you tomorrow, God willing.

75. *Odyssey* XVII, 347. (Telemachus refers to the disguised Odysseus.)
The same passage is quoted at *Charmides* 161A.

Charmides

Introduction

Although the *Charmides,* with its inquiry into the nature of a single virtue, temperance, has obvious affinities with the *Laches* and with other early dialogues, the complexities of its latter pages bear more resemblance to the aridities of the *Theaetetus* and *Parmenides* than to dialogues of the early group. Nevertheless, the main theme, the connection between virtue and knowledge, is the same as that of the *Laches.* And, as courage in the *Laches* tended to remove itself from what I call the first-order level of the various arts and techniques such as flute playing or medicine, so temperance in the *Charmides* does the same thing. Plato has come to realize that to state this point more decisively is also to state it more subtly. By associating virtue with knowledge he has involved himself in the mechanics of the term "knowledge" as well as in the question of defining the various virtues. "Knowledge" (or "science") is in fact a *tinos*-word. To use it is to raise the question "knowledge of what?" On the first-order level, the answer to this is easy—medicine is knowledge of health, and cobbling, of shoes. But it always remains possible for these techniques to be misused, or, to put it another way, efficiency is not always goodness. How is Plato, with his concern for good government, to assure that the first-order arts are regularly employed for good ends? His answer is basically simple: by having them ruled over by a second-order art that is in itself an art of goodness. (Later, in the *Republic,* he will express the same thought by stipulating that in the good state the philosopher shall be king.) But his way of presenting this answer is not simple. True to the Socratic procedure, he forces the reader to reach the solution himself. So he hammers away at the analogy of the art of temperance (a science of sciences, the knowledge of good and evil) with the first-order arts, in the hope that by so doing he will demonstrate both its likeness to them (both are "of" something) and its difference from them (temperance is a second-order art ruling over arts of the first order). Plato has no desire to make a total separation between the two kinds of art. Not only will there always be a close relationship between ruler and ruled, but he still cherishes the notion that somehow there should be teachers of good and evil in the same way that there are teachers of cobbling and carpentry. When Socrates went about Athens looking for someone wiser than himself, he admired the craftsmen most (*Apology* 22D). The method of teaching first and second-order arts cannot be the same (we can see this by imagining a University course in first-year Goodness), but he clings to the notion that any form of genuine knowledge *must* be teachable. If we think again of his preoccupation with good government (which is really the problem of producing good men), we can see that for him the problem becomes acute.

If the student will bear these points in mind, I believe he can approach the *Charmides* with some confidence. The setting and characters are handled with greater artistic skill than in the *Laches,* so that the dialogue is initially much more readable. The chief remaining difficulty is the severity of the Socratic *elenchus.* Plato has mounted such a strong attack upon the notion of temperance as the knowledge of good and evil that it is hard to believe that he really intends the reader to accept it. That he does so intend is something that I hope to have made clear in the notes.

Persons of the "Charmides"

Charmides is Plato's own uncle, the brother of Plato's mother, Perictione. He was, with his relative and guardian Critias, a member of the Thirty Tyrants of 404. Both men fell in battle in 403 when the democrats returned. He also appears at *Protagoras* 314E and *Symposium* 222B.

Critias, a first cousin of Plato's mother, Perictione, and born about 460, is an older and more prominent person than Charmides. He also became a member of the Thirty and fell in the fighting of 403. In addition, he was a literary figure associated with the sophists. The remains of his writings may be seen in Diels-Kranz, *Die Fragmente der Vorsokratiker.* § 88.

Chaerephon is the devoted disciple of Socrates who put the important question to the Delphic oracle (is there anyone wiser than Socrates?) reported in the *Apology* at 21Aff. It seems to have been this episode which started Socrates on his philosophic mission. Chaerephon's brief appearance in the *Charmides* shows us his Socratic fanaticism (153Bff.) and is appropriate in view of the attention given in the dialogue to the Delphic maxim "Know thyself" (164Dff.). He makes another brief appearance at the beginning of the *Gorgias* 447Aff., where he conducts a short Socratic discussion with Polus (448BC).

Socrates is about 37, considerably younger than he is in the *Laches.*

Dramatic Date

The dramatic date is fixed by the mention (153A) of the events at Potidaea in 432.

Selected Bibliography

BURNET, JOHN, ed. *Platonis Opera*, vol. 3. "Oxford Classical Texts." Oxford 1903. Reprinted 1957.

CROISET, ALFRED, ed. *Charmide*, in "Collection des Universités de France." Budé Edition, vol. 2. Paris, 1965.

FRIEDLÄNDER, PAUL. *Plato: The Dialogues (First Period)*. Translated by Hans Meyerhoff. New York, 1964. Pp. 67–81.

GUTHRIE, W. K. C. *A History of Greek Philosophy* IV. Cambridge: Cambridge, 1975. Pp. 199–212.

NORTH, HELEN. *Sophrosyne: Self-Knowledge and Self-Restraint in Greek Literature*. Ithaca, 1966. Pp. 153–158.

SHOREY, PAUL. *What Plato Said*. Chicago, 1933. Pp. 100–105.

SPRAGUE, ROSAMOND KENT. *Plato's Philosopher-King*. Columbia: South Carolina, 1976. Chapter III, "The *Charmides*."

TAYLOR, A. E. *Plato: The Man and His Work*. London, 1926, (6th edition reprinted 1949). Pp. 47–57.

TELOH, HENRY. *Socratic Education in Plato's Early Dialogues*. Notre Dame, Indiana: Notre Dame, 1986. Chapter IV. "Natural Virtue and Education in the *Charmides*."

TUCKEY, T. G. *Plato's Charmides*. Cambridge, 1951.

VAN DER BEN, N. *The "Charmides" of Plato: Problems and Interpretations*. Amsterdam, 1985.

WATT, DONALD. Translation with introduction and notes. *Early Socratic Dialogues*. ed. Trevor J. Saunders. New York: Penguin Classics, 1987.

WEST, THOMAS G. and GRACE STARRY WEST. Translation with introduction and notes. Indianapolis: Hackett, 1986.

Charmides

We got back the preceding evening from the camp at Potidaea,[1] and since I was arriving after such a long absence I sought out my accustomed haunts with special pleasure. To be more specific, I went straight to the palaestra of Taureas[2] (the one directly opposite the temple of Basile)[3], and there I found a good number of people, most of whom were familiar, though there were some, too, whom I didn't know. When they saw me coming in unexpectedly, I was immediately hailed at a distance by people coming up from all directions, and Chaerephon, like the wild man he is, sprang up from the midst of a group of people and ran towards me and, seizing me by the hand, exclaimed, "Socrates! how did you come off in the battle?" (A short time before we came away there had been a battle at Potidaea and the people at home had only just got the news.)

And I said in reply, "Exactly as you see me."

"The way we heard it here," he said, "the fighting was very heavy and many of our friends were killed."

---

1. Potidaea was a Corinthian colony in the Chalcidian peninsula which revolted from the Delian Confederacy in 432. It was reduced to submission by a large force of Athenian hoplites. For Plato's description of Socrates' behavior in the camp and in the battle, see the speech of Alcibiades in the *Symposium* 219Eff.
2. This Taureas is the man assaulted by Alcibiades. See Plutarch *Alcibiades* 16, Demosthenes *Midias* 147, and J. K. Davies, *Athenian Propertied Families 600-300 B.C.* (Oxford, 1971), p. 29.
3. A sanctuary sacred to Codrus, Neleus, and Basile is mentioned in a Greek inscription (*IG*2, 94). Basile seems to have been a personification of Athenian royalty.

"The report is pretty accurate," I said.

"Were you actually in the battle?" he said.

"Yes, I was there."

"Well, come sit down and give us a complete account, because we've had very few details so far." And while he was still talking he brought me over to Critias, the son of Callaeschrus, and sat me down there.

153D When I took my seat I greeted Critias and the rest and proceeded to relate the news from the camp in answer to whatever questions anyone asked, and they asked plenty of different ones.

When they had had enough of these things, I in my turn began to question them with respect to affairs at home, about the present state of philosophy and about the young men, whether there were any who had become distinguished for wisdom or beauty or both. Whereupon Critias, glancing

154A towards the door and seeing several young men coming in and laughing with each other, with a crowd of others following behind, said "As far as beauty goes, Socrates, I think you will be able to make up your mind straight away, because those coming in are the advance party and the admirers of the one who is thought to be the handsomest young man of the day, and I think that he himself cannot be far off."

"But who is he," I said, "and who is his father?"

"You probably know him," he said, "but he was not yet

B grown up when you went away.⁴ He is Charmides, the son of my mother's brother Glaucon, and my cousin."

"Good heavens, of course I know him," I said, "because he was worth noticing even when he was a child. By now I suppose he must be pretty well grown up."

"It won't be long," he said, "before you discover how grown up he is and how he has turned out." And while he was speaking Charmides came in.

---

4. Socrates would seem to have been on campaign for some considerable time. Cf. 156A.

You mustn't judge by me, my friend. I'm a broken yard-stick[5] as far as handsome people are concerned, because practically everyone of that age strikes me as beautiful. But even so, at the moment Charmides came in he seemed to me to be 154C amazing in stature and appearance, and everyone there looked to me to be in love with him, they were so astonished and confused by his entrance, and many other lovers followed in his train. That men of my age should have been affected this way was natural enough, but I noticed that even the small boys fixed their eyes upon him and no one of them, not even the littlest, looked at anyone else, but all gazed at him as if he were a statue. And Chaerephon called to me and said, "Well, Socrates, what do you think of the young man? Hasn't he a splendid D face?"

"Extraordinary," I said.

"But if he were willing to strip," he said, "you would hardly notice his face, his body is so perfect."

Well, everyone else said the same things as Chaerephon, and I said, "By Heracles, you are describing a man without an equal—if he should happen to have one small thing in addition."

"What's that?" asked Critias.

"If he happens to have a well-formed soul," I said. "It would be appropriate if he did, Critias, since he comes from your family."[6]

"He is very distinguished in that respect too," he said.

"Then why don't we undress this part of him and have a look at it before we inspect his body? Surely he has already reached the age when he is willing to discuss things."

"Very much so," said Critias, "since he is not only a philosopher but also, both in his own opinion and that of others, quite a poet." 155A

5. Literally, a "white line", which would not show up on, say, white marble. Hence the stonemason would use something colored. Cf. the Scholiast, ad loc.

6. And, of course, from Plato's own family, since Charmides is his own maternal uncle. Cf. 157E below.

"This is a gift, my dear Critias," I said, "which has been in your family as far back as Solon.[7] But why not call the young man over and put him through his paces? Even though he is still so young, there can be nothing wrong in talking to him when you are here, since you are both his guardian and his cousin."

"You are right," he said; "we'll call him." And he imme-
155B diately spoke to his servant and said, "Boy, call Charmides and tell him I want him to meet a doctor for the weakness he told me he was suffering from yesterday." Then Critias said to me, "You see, just lately he's complained of a headache when he gets up in the morning. Why not pretend to him that you know a remedy for it?"[8]

"No reason why not," I said, "if he will only come."

"Oh, he will come," he said.

Which is just what happened. He did come, and his com-
C ing caused a lot of laughter, because every one of us who was already seated began pushing hard at his neighbor so as to make a place for him to sit down. The upshot of it was that we made the man sitting at one end get up, and the man at the other end was toppled off sideways. In the end he came and sat down between me and Critias.[9] And then, my friend, I really was in difficulties, and although I had thought it would be perfectly easy to talk to him, I found my previous brash confidence quite gone. And when Critias said that I was the per-
D son who knew the remedy and he turned his full gaze upon me in a manner beyond description and seemed on the point of asking a question, and when everyone in the palaestra surged all around us in a circle, then, my noble friend, I saw inside his cloak and caught on fire and was quite beside myself. And it occurred to me that Cydias[10] was the wisest love-poet when he gave someone advice on the subject of beautiful boys and said that "the fawn should beware lest, while taking a

7. Athenian poet and lawgiver of the early sixth century. Cf. *Laches* 188B and 189A.
8. Critias is engaging in a piece of deceit, but there is of course a sense in which Socrates is a physician—of the soul.
9. Similar scenes occur at *Lysis* 207AB and at *Euthydemus* 274BC.
10. Cydias appears to be otherwise unknown.

look at the lion, he should provide part of the lion's dinner,"
because I felt as if I had been snapped up by such a creature.
All the same, when he asked me if I knew the headache remedy, I managed somehow to answer that I did.[11]

"What exactly is it?" he said.

And I said that it was a certain leaf, and that there was a **155E**
charm to go with it. If one sang the charm while applying
the leaf, the remedy would bring about a complete cure, but
without the charm the leaf was useless.[12]

And he said, "Well, then I shall write down the charm **156A**
at your dictation."

"With my permission," I said, "or without it?"

"With it, of course, Socrates," he said, laughing.

"Very well," I said. "And are you quite sure about my
name?"

"It would be disgraceful if I were not," he said, "because
you are no small topic of conversation among us boys, and be-
sides, I remember you being with Critias here when I was a
child."

"Good for you," I said. "Then I shall speak more freely
about the nature of the charm. Just now I was in difficulties **B**
about what method I would adopt in order to demonstrate
its power to you. Its nature, Charmides, is not such as to be
able to cure the head alone. You have probably heard this
about good doctors, that if you go to them with a pain in
the eyes, they are likely to say that they cannot undertake to
cure the eyes by themselves, but that it will be necessary to
treat the head at the same time if things are also to go well
with the eyes. And again it would be very foolish to suppose **C**
that one could ever treat the head by itself without treating
the whole body. In keeping with this principle, they plan a

11. It may be relevant to note that in the *Symposium* 210Aff., the love
of Beauty begins with the love of one beautiful boy. Note also that Socrates here shows himself in possession of the virtue, self-control or temperance, which is about to be discussed.

12. For a fascinating study of the use of charms in medicine see P.
Laín Entralgo, *The Therapy of the Word in Classical Antiquity*, trans.
Rather and Sharp (New Haven, 1970). Pp. 108-128 contain a discussion
of the *Charmides*.

regime for the whole body with the idea of treating and curing the part along with the whole. Or haven't you noticed that this is what they say and what the situation is?"

"Yes, I have," he said.

"Then what I have said appears true, and you accept the principle?"

"Absolutely," he said.

156D   And when I heard his approval, I took heart and, little by little, my former confidence revived, and I began to wake up. So I said, "Well, Charmides, it is just the same with this charm. I learned it while I was with the army, from one of the Thracian doctors of Zalmoxis,[13] who are also said to make men immortal. And this Thracian said that the Greek doctors were right to say what I told you just now. 'But our king Zalmoxis,' he said, 'who is a god, says that just as one should

E   not attempt to cure the eyes apart from the head, nor the head apart from the body, so one should not attempt to cure the body apart from the soul.[14] And this, he says, is the very reason why most diseases are beyond the Greek doctors, that they do not pay attention to the whole as they ought to do, since if the whole is not in good condition, it is impossible that the part should be. Because,' he said, 'the soul is the source both of bodily health and bodily disease for the whole man, and these flow from the soul in the same way that the eyes are affected by the head. So it is necessary first and foremost to cure the

157A   soul if the parts of the head and of the rest of the body are to be healthy. And the soul,' he said, 'my dear friend, is cured by means of certain charms, and these charms consist of beautiful words. It is a result of such words that temperance[15] arises

13. Herodotus IV, 94-96 tells us that Zalmoxis was a god of the dead among a Thracian tribe, the Getae. Nothing is known about any Thracian doctors beyond the present passage.

14. This is the important step.

15. The word translated "temperance" (*sōphrosyne*) carries associations of sound-mindedness, prudence, and self-knowledge which are almost impossible to convey in English. For an excellent study of the concept see Helen North, *Sophrosyne: Self-Knowledge and Self-Restraint in Greek Literature* (Ithaca, 1966). Pp. 153-158 are devoted to the *Charmides*.

in the soul, and when the soul acquires and possesses temperance, it is easy to provide health both for the head and for the rest of the body.' So when he taught me the remedy and the charms, he also said, 'Don't let anyone persuade you to treat his head with this remedy who does not first submit his soul to you for treatment with the charm. Because nowadays,' he said, 'this is the mistake some doctors make with their patients. They try to produce health of body apart from health of soul.' And he gave me very strict instructions that I should be deaf to the entreaties of wealth, position, and personal beauty. So I (for I have given him my promise and must keep it) shall be obedient, and if you are willing, in accordance with the stranger's instructions, to submit your soul to be charmed with the Thracian's charms first, then I shall apply the remedy to your head. But if not, there is nothing we can do for you, my dear Charmides."

157B

C

When Critias heard me saying this, he said, "The headache will turn out to have been a lucky thing for the young man, Socrates, if, because of his head, he will be forced to improve his wits.[16] Let me tell you, though, that Charmides not only outstrips his contemporaries in beauty of form but also in this very thing for which you say you have the charm; it was temperance, wasn't it?"

D

"Yes, indeed it was," I said.

"Then you must know that not only does he have the reputation of being the most temperate young man of the day, but that he is second to none in everything else appropriate to his age."

"And it is quite right, Charmides, that you should be superior to the rest in all such things," I replied, "because I don't suppose that anyone else here could so readily point to two Athenian families whose union would be likely to produce a more aristocratic lineage than that from which you are sprung. Your father's family, that of Critias, the son of Dropi-

E

---

16. Critias has not quite understood Socrates.

des,[17] has been praised for us by Anacreon,[18] Solon, and many other poets for superior beauty, virtue, and everything else called happiness. It's the same on your mother's side. Your maternal uncle Pyrilampes[19] has the reputation of being the finest and most influential man in the country because of his numerous embassies to the Great King[20] and others, so that this whole side of the family is not a bit inferior to the other. As the offspring of such forebears, it is likely that you hold pride of place. In the matter of visible beauty, dear son of Glaucon, you appear to me to be in no respect surpassed by those who come before. But if, in addition, you have a sufficient share of temperance and the other attributes mentioned by your friend here, then your mother bore a blessed son in you, my dear Charmides. Now this is the situation: if temperance is already present in you, as Critias here asserts, and if you are sufficiently temperate, you have no need of the charms either of Zalmoxis or of Abaris the Hyperborean,[21] and you may have the remedy for the head straightaway. But if you still appear to lack these things, you must be charmed before you are given the remedy. So tell me yourself: do you agree with your friend and assert that you already partake sufficiently of temperance, or would you say that you are lacking in it?"

At first Charmides blushed and looked more beautiful than ever, and his bashfulness was becoming at his age. Then he answered in a way that was quite dignified: he said that it was not easy for him, in the present circumstances, either to agree or to disagree with what had been asked. "Because," he said, "if I should deny that I am temperate, it would not only

17. This Critias is the grandfather of our Critias. (See *Timaeus* 20E.) But see J. K. Davies, *Athenian Propertied Families 600-300 B.C.* (Oxford, 1971), pp. 324-326.

18. Lyric poet born in Teos about 570 B.C.

19. Friend of Pericles and stepfather of Plato. He was famous for breeding peacocks.

20. That is, to the King of the Persians.

21. Herodotus (IV, 36) says he is *not* going to tell the story of Abaris, who carried an arrow through the whole world while fasting. Abaris seems to have been a semilegendary person, a servant of Apollo.

seem an odd thing to say about oneself, but I would at the same time make Critias here a liar, and so with the many others to whom, by his account, I appear to be temperate. But if, on the other hand, I should agree and should praise myself, perhaps that would appear distasteful. So I do not know what I am to answer."

And I said, "What you say appears to me to be reasonable, Charmides. And I think," I said, "we ought to investigate together the question whether you do or do not possess the thing I am inquiring about, so that you will not be forced to say anything against your will and I, on the other hand, shall not turn to doctoring in an irresponsible way. If this is agreeable to you, I would like to investigate the question with you, but if not, we can give it up."

158E

"Oh, I should like it above all things," he said, "so go ahead and investigate the matter in whatever way you think best."

"Well then," I said, "in these circumstances, I think the following method would be best. Now it is clear that if temperance is present[22] in you, you have some opinion about it. Because it is necessary, I suppose, that if it really resides in you, it provides a sense of its presence, by means of which you would form an opinion not only that you have it but of what sort it is. Or don't you think so?"

159A

"Yes," he said, "I do think so."

"Well, then, since you know how to speak Greek," I said, "I suppose you could express this impression of yours in just the way it strikes you?"[23]

"Perhaps," he said.

---

22. Here and at 160D and 161A Socrates uses the verb *pareinai*, later to become part of the technical vocabulary of the theory of Forms. (For a survey of this vocabulary, see W. D. Ross, *Plato's Theory of Ideas*. [Oxford, 1951], pp. 228-229. Ross does not list any passages from the *Charmides*, however.)

23. In Socrates' view, those who possess a virtue should be able to define it. It is for this reason, presumably, that in the *Laches* it is a pair of generals who are asked to say what courage is.

"Well, to help us decide whether it resides in you or not, say what, in your opinion, temperance is," I said.

159B At first he shied away and was rather unwilling to answer. Finally, however, he said that in his opinion temperance was doing everything in an orderly and quiet way—things like walking in the streets, and talking, and doing everything else in a similar fashion. "So I think," he said, "taking it all together, that what you ask about is a sort of quietness."[24]

"Perhaps you are right," I said, "at least they do say, Charmides, that the quiet are temperate.[25] Let's see if there
C is anything in it. Tell me, temperance is one of the admirable things, isn't it?"[26]

"Yes indeed," he said.

"Now when you are at the writing master's, is it more admirable to copy the letters quickly or quietly?"[27]

"Quickly."

"What about reading? Quickly or quietly?"

"Quickly."

"And certainly to play the lyre quickly and to wrestle in a lively fashion is much more admirable than to do these things quietly and slowly?"

"Yes."

"Well, isn't the same thing true about boxing and the pancration?"

"Yes indeed."

"And with running and jumping and all the movements

24. It should be noted that Charmides does not require the same instruction in the nature of definition as, for instance, Laches. (190Eff., and cf. *Meno* 71Eff, *Theaetetus* 146Eff.)

25. Note that Socrates, as often, moves from the quality to the persons possessing it without any apparent sense of incongruity. Note also that we cannot tell whether he takes the quiet to be a subclass of the temperate or coextensive with them.

26. Cf. the similar step at *Laches* 192C.

27. In English we would not expect "quickly" as the opposite of "quietly", but the Greek word *hēsuchei* connotes slowness as well as quietness. Socrates may be deliberately exploiting this ambiguity for the purposes of his argument. See below on 160B.

of the body, aren't the ones that are performed briskly and quickly the admirable ones, and those performed with difficulty and quietly the ugly ones?"

"It seems so."

"And it seems to us that, in matters of the body, it is not the quieter movement but the quickest and most lively which is the most admirable. Isn't it so?"

"Yes indeed."

"But temperance was something admirable?"

"Yes."

"Then in the case of the body it would not be quietness but quickness which is the more temperate, since temperance is an admirable thing."

"That seems reasonable," he said.

"Well then," I said, "is facility in learning more admirable or difficulty in learning?"[28]

"Facility."

"But facility in learning is learning quickly? And difficulty in learning is learning quietly and slowly?"

"Yes."

"And to teach another person quickly—isn't this far more admirable than to teach him quietly and slowly?"

"Yes."

"Well then, to recall and to remember quietly and slowly—is this more admirable, or to do it vehemently and quickly?"

"Vehemently," he said, "and quickly."

"And isn't shrewdness a kind of liveliness of soul, and not a kind of quietness?"

"True."

"And again this is also true of understanding what is said, at the writing master's and at the lyre teacher's and everywhere else: to act not as quietly but as quickly as possible is the most admirable."

28. Although the refutation appears to be finished, Socrates wants to make the same points for soul as for body.

"Yes."

"And, further, in the operations of thought and in making plans, it is not the quietest man, I think, and the man who plans and finds out things with difficulty who appears to be 160B   worthy of praise but the one who does these things most easily and quickly."

"Exactly so," he said.

"Therefore, Charmides," I said, "in all these cases, both of soul and body, we think that quickness and speed are more admirable than slowness and quietness?"

"It seems likely," he said.

"We conclude then that temperance would not be a kind of quietness, nor would the temperate life be quiet, as far as this argument is concerned at any rate,[29] since the temperate life is necessarily an admirable thing. There are two possi-
C   bilities for us: either no quiet actions in life appear to be more admirable than the swift and strong ones, or very few. If then, my friend, even quite a few quiet actions should turn out to be more admirable than the violent and quick ones, not even on this assumption would temperance consist in doing things quietly rather than in doing them violently and quickly, neither in walking nor in speech nor in anything else; nor would the quiet life be more temperate than its oppo-
D   site, since in the course of the argument we placed temperance among the admirable things, and the quick things have turned out to be no less admirable than the quiet ones."

"What you say seems to me quite right, Socrates," he said.

"Then start over again, Charmides," I said, "and look into yourself with greater concentration, and when you have decided what effect the presence of temperance has upon you and what sort of thing it must be to have this effect, then put

29. Socrates may be calling our attention to the fact that the refutation depended on taking "quietness" in a sense which Charmides did not intend.

all this together[30] and tell me clearly and bravely, what does it 160E
appear to you to be?"

He paused and, looking into himself very manfully, said,
"Well, temperance seems to me to make people ashamed and
bashful, and so I think modesty must be what temperance
really is."

"But," I said, "didn't we agree just now that temperance
was an admirable thing?"

"Yes, we did," he said.

"And it would follow that temperate men are good?"

"Yes."

"And could a thing be good that does not produce good
men?"[31]

"Of course not."

"Then not only is temperance an admirable thing, but
it is a good thing."

"I agree." 161A

"Well then," I said, "you don't agree with Homer when
he said that 'modesty is not a good mate for a needy man'?"[32]

"Oh, but I do," he said.

"So it seems to be the case that modesty both is and is not
a good."

"Yes, it does."

"But temperance must be a good if it makes those good
in whom it is present and makes bad those in whom it is not."

"Why yes, it seems to me to be exactly as you say."

"Then temperance would not be modesty if it really is
a good and if modesty is no more good than bad." B

---

30. Literally, "syllogize". On this passage see Richard Robinson, *Plato's
Earlier Dialectic*, 2nd ed. (Oxford, 1953), p. 21: "The verb 'syllogize'
occurs in the *Charmides* (160D), not as something to be done towards the
end of an elenchus, but as something to be done in formulating a thesis:
you form the thesis by syllogizing or putting together the relevant facts".

31. It is axiomatic for Plato that the good is productive (and useful).
See, for instance, *Meno* 87E.

32. *Odyssey* XVII, 347. (Telemachus refers to the disguised Odysseus.)
The same passage is quoted at *Laches* 201B.

"What you say has quite convinced me, Socrates," he said. "But give me your opinion of the following definition of temperance: I have just remembered having heard someone say that temperance is minding one's own business.[33] Tell me if you think the person who said this was right."

And I said, "You wretch, you've picked this up from Critias or from some other wise man."

161C

"I guess it was from some other," said Critias, because it was certainly not from me."[34]

"What difference does it make, Socrates," said Charmides, "from whom I heard it?"

"None at all," I answered, "since the question at issue is not who said it, but whether what he said is true or not."

"Now I like what you say," he said.

"Good for you," I replied, "but if we succeed in finding out what it means, I should be surprised, because it seems to be a sort of riddle."

"In what way?" he asked.

D

"I mean," I said, "that when he uttered the words, I don't suppose the person speaking really meant that temperance was minding your own business. Or do you consider that the writing master does nothing when he writes or reads?"

"On the contrary, I do think he does something."

"And do you think the writing master teaches you to read and write your own name only or those of the other boys as well? And do you write the names of your enemies just as much as your own names and those of your friends?"

---

33. Literally, "to do the things of oneself" (*to ta heautou prattein*). The Greeks particularly disliked the meddler in other people's affairs. (See V. Ehrenberg, "Polypragmosyne: A Study in Greek Politics," *Journal of Hellenic Studies* LXVII [1947]: 46-67.) It is noteworthy that although the notion of minding one's own business is ridiculed here in the *Charmides*, it is taken seriously in the *Republic*, e.g. 433A, where it turns out to be the definition of justice. There, of course, the expression is taken in the sense of doing the work for which one is best fitted.

34. But see below 162C.

"Just as much," he said.

"And are you a busybody and intemperate when you do   161E
this?"

"Not at all."

"But aren't you doing other people's business if to read
and write are to do something?"

"I suppose I am."

"And then healing, my friend, is doing something, I suppose, and so is housebuilding and weaving and engaging in
any one of the arts."

"Yes indeed."

"Well then," I said, "do you think a city would be well
governed by a law commanding each man to weave and wash
his own cloak, make his own shoes and oil flask and scraper,
and perform everything else by this same principle of keeping   162A
his hands off of other people's things and making and doing
his own?"

"No, I don't think it would," he said.

"But," said I, "if a city is going to be temperately governed, it must be governed well."

"Of course," he said.

"Then if temperance is 'minding your own business', it
can't be minding things of this sort and in this fashion."

"Apparently not."

"Then the person who said that temperance was 'minding your own business' must, apparently, have been riddling,
as I pointed out just now, because I don't suppose he was quite
so simpleminded. Or was it some silly fellow you heard say-   B
ing this, Charmides?"

"Far from it," he said, "he seemed very wise indeed."

"Then I think he must certainly have tossed off a riddle,
since it is difficult to know what in the world this 'minding
your own business' can be."

"Perhaps it is," he said.

"Then what in the world is 'minding your own business'?
Are you able to say?"

"I'm at a total loss," he said. "But perhaps the one who said it didn't know what he meant either." And when he said this he smiled and looked at Critias.

162C   It was clear that Critias had been agitated for some time and also that he was eager to impress Charmides and the rest who were there. He had held himself in with difficulty earlier, but now he could do so no longer. In my opinion, what I suspected earlier was certainly true, that Charmides had picked up this saying about temperance from Critias. And then Charmides, who wanted the author of the definition to take over the argument rather than himself, tried to provoke him to it

D   by going on pointing out that the cause was lost. Critias couldn't put up with this but seemed to me to be angry with Charmides just the way a poet is when his verse is mangled by the actors. So he gave him a look and said, "Do you suppose, Charmides, that just because *you* don't understand what in the world the man meant who said that temperance was 'minding your own business', the man himself doesn't understand either?"

"Well, my dear Critias," said I, "there would be nothing

E   remarkable in his being ignorant of the matter at his age, but you, because of your age and experience, are very likely to understand it. So if you agree that temperance is what the man said it was and take over the argument, I would be very happy to investigate with you the question whether what was said is true or not."

"I am quite ready to agree," he said, "and to take over the argument."

"I admire you for it," I said. "Now tell me: do you also agree with what I was just saying, that all craftsmen make something?"[35]

35. If Socrates refers to 161E, he has not said exactly this, since he there speaks of "doing" (*prattein*) rather than "making" (*poiein*). The two are often very close in meaning, but he seems to want to force Critias to distinguish clearly between them, as Critias proceeds to do at 163A below. (My guess is that Plato, who wants to use the expression seriously in the *Republic*, would like to make it more precise and, perhaps, to get rid of the notion of product.)

"Yes I do."

"And do they seem to you to make their own things only,   163A
or those of other people as well?"

"Those of others as well."

"And are they temperate in not making their own things
only?"

"Is there any objection?" he asked.

"None for me," I said, "but see whether there may not be
one for the man who defines temperance as 'minding your
own business' and then says there is no objection if those who
do other people's business are temperate too."

"But," said he, "have I agreed that those who *do* other
people's business are temperate by admitting that those *making* other people's things are temperate?"[36]

"Tell me," I said, "don't you call making and doing the   B
same thing?"

"Not at all," he said, "nor do I call working and making
the same.[37] I have learned this from Hesiod, who said 'work is
no disgrace'.[38] Do you suppose that Hesiod, if he referred to
the sort of things you mentioned just now by both the term
'work' and the term 'do', would have said there was no disgrace
in cobbling or selling salt fish or prostitution? One ought not

36. Critias has perceived that Socrates has announced a refutation of
"doing" (*prattein*) by means of an argument based on "making"
(*poiein*).

37. Critias, apparently foreseeing a further move by Socrates, proceeds
to distinguish "working" (*ergazesthai*) from "making" (*poiein*). His idea
seems to be that if Socrates is capable of equating *poiein* with *prattein*
(see previous note), he will be equally capable of equating *poiein* with
ergazesthai and then *ergazesthai* with *prattein*. (That is, having failed in
a direct equation of *poiein* and *prattein* he will try an indirect one.)
Critias would not object to the identity of *ergazesthai* and *prattein* so long
as *poiein* remains separate from both. He is apparently afraid that Socrates will include all sorts of unaristocratic activities under that heading.

38. *Works and Days* 311. It is interesting to note that at Xenophon
Memorabilia I, 2, 56, Socrates is reported to have been accused of just
the misinterpretation of this passage to which Critias now objects. Further,
Critias here supplies the correction, that Hesiod referred to the doing of
good works only, which Xenophon says was supplied by Socrates. Perhaps
Plato wants to show by a specific illustration that the pupils of Socrates
were not corrupted by their teacher.

to think this, Socrates, but rather believe, as I do, that he supposed making to be something other than doing and working,
163C   and that a 'made' or created thing became a disgrace on those
occasions when it was not accompanied by the admirable, but
that work is never any sort of disgrace. Because he gave the
name 'works' to things done admirably and usefully, and it is
creations of this sort which are 'works' and 'actions'. We ought
to represent him as thinking that only things of this sort are
'one's own' and that all the harmful ones belong to other
people. The result is that we must suppose that Hesiod and
any other man of sense calls the man who minds his own business temperate."

D   "Critias," I said, "I understood the beginning of your
speech pretty well, when you said that you called things that
were 'one's own' and 'of oneself' good and called the doing of
good things actions, because I have heard Prodicus[39] discourse
upon the distinctions in words a hundred times. Well, I give
you permission to define each word the way you like just so
long as you make clear the application of whatever word you
use.[40] Now start at the beginning and define more clearly: the
E   doing of good things or the making of them or whatever you
want to call it—is this what you say temperance is?"

"Yes, it is," he said.

"And the man who performs evil actions is not temperate, but the man who performs good ones?"[41]

"Doesn't it seem so to you, my friend?"

"Never mind that," I said; "we are not investigating what
I think but rather what you now say."

"Well then, I," he said, "deny that the man who does
things that are not good but bad is temperate, and assert that
the man who does things that are good but not bad *is* temper-

39. See on *Laches* 197D.
40. The foregoing could well serve as an accurate account of Plato's
attitude towards technical philosophical terminology.
41. The upshot of the previous discussion is now apparent: Critias'
definition will need to bring in the question of value. Critias realized
this himself (163C), but there will be a basic disagreement between him
and Socrates as to what the admirable and useful really are.

ate. So I give you a clear definition of temperance as the doing of good things."

"And there is no reason why you should not be speak- 164A ing the truth. But it certainly does surprise me," I said, "if you believe that temperate men are ignorant of their temperance."⁴²

"I don't think so at all," he said.

"But didn't you say just a moment ago," said I, "that there was nothing to prevent craftsmen, even while they do other people's business, from being temperate?"

"Yes, I did say that," he said. "But what about it?"

"Nothing, but tell me if you think that a doctor, when he makes someone healthy, does something useful both for himself and for the person he cures." B

"Yes, I agree."

"And the man who does these things does what he ought?"⁴³

"Yes."

"And the man who does what he ought is temperate, isn't he?"

"Of course he is temperate."

"And does a doctor have to know when he cures in a useful way and when he does not?⁴⁴ And so with each of the craftsmen: does he have to know when he is going to benefit from the work he performs and when he is not?"

"Perhaps not."

"Then sometimes," I said, "the doctor doesn't know himself whether he has acted beneficially or harmfully. Now if he C

---

42. This is a crucial step, since it will lead to the discussion of self-knowledge at 165Cff. The transition would sound less odd to a Greek than it does to us; see on 157A.

43. Socrates is not speaking of duty, but of what is necessary to be done.

44. In other words, there may be an element of self-knowledge involved in the performance of useful actions. The doctor sometimes knows himself as doing what is useful as well as knowing what is in fact useful. (The former type of knowledge would be second-order; see Preface pp. viii-ix) .

has acted beneficially, then, according to your argument, he has acted temperately. Or isn't this what you said?"

"Yes, it is."

"Then it seems that on some occasions he acts beneficially and, in so doing, acts temperately and is temperate, but is ignorant of his own temperance?"

"But this," he said, "Socrates, would never happen. And if you think it necessary to draw this conclusion from what I D admitted before, then I would rather withdraw some of my statements, and would not be ashamed to admit I had made a mistake, in preference to conceding that a man ignorant of himself could be temperate. As a matter of fact, this is pretty much what I say temperance is, to know oneself, and I agree with the inscription to this effect set up at Delphi.[45] Because this inscription appears to me to have been dedicated for the following purpose, as though it were a greeting from the god to those coming in in place of the usual 'Hail', as though to E say 'hail' were an incorrect greeting, but we should rather urge one another to 'be temperate'. It is in this fashion, then, that the god greets those who enter his temple, not after the manner of man—or so I suppose the man thought who dedicated the inscription. What he says to the person entering is nothing else than 'be temperate'; this is what he says. Now in saying this he speaks very darkly, as a seer would do. That 165A 'know thyself' and 'be temperate' are the same (as the inscription claims, and so do I) might be doubted by some, and this I think to be the case with those who dedicated the later inscriptions 'Nothing too much' and 'Pledges lead to perdition'. Because these people thought that 'Know thyself' was a piece of advice and not the god's greeting to those who enter, so, with the idea of dedicating some admonitions which were no less useful, they wrote these things and put them up. But here's the reason why I say all this, Socrates: I concede to you B everything that was said before—perhaps you said something

45. According to Croiset (Budé edition, ad loc.) the inscription was probably intended to mean something like, "realize your mortal condition."

more nearly right on the subject and perhaps I did, but nothing of what we said was really clear—but now I wish to give you an explanation of this definition, unless of course you already agree that temperance is to know oneself."

"But Critias," I replied, "you are talking to me as though I professed to know the answers to my own questions and as though I could agree with you if I really wished. This is not the case—rather, because of my own ignorance, I am continually investigating in your company whatever is put forward. However, if I think it over, I am willing to say whether I agree or not. Just wait while I consider."

165C

"Well, think it over," he said.

"Yes, I'm thinking," said I. "Well, if knowing is what temperance is, then it clearly must be some sort of science and must be of something,[46] isn't that so?"

"Yes—of oneself," he said.

"Then medicine, too," I said, "is a science and is of health?"

"Certainly."

"Now," I said, "if you should ask me, 'If medicine is a science of health, what benefit does it confer upon us and what does it produce'?, I would answer that it conferred no small benefit. Because health is a fine result for us, if you agree that this is what it produces."

D

"I agree."

"And if you should ask me about housebuilding, which is a science of building houses, and ask what I say that it produces, I would say that it produces houses, and so on with the other arts. So you ought to give an answer on behalf of temperance, since you say it is a science of self, in case you should be asked, 'Critias, since temperance is a science of self, what fine result does it produce which is worthy of the name?' Come along, tell me."

E

46. In other words, science (*epistēmē*) is a *tinos*-word. (See Preface pp. viii-ix). We are about to get the familiar type of paradox generated by combining first- and second-order *technai*. Cf. *Protagoras* 312DE.

"But, Socrates," he said, "you are not conducting the investigation in the right way. This science does not have the same nature as the rest, any more than they have the same nature as each other, but you are carrying on the investigation as though they were all the same.[47] For instance," he said, "in the arts of calculation and geometry, tell me what is the product corresponding to the house in the case of housebuilding and the cloak in the case of weaving and so on—one could give many instances from many arts. You ought to point out to me a similar product in these cases, but you won't be able to do it."

166A

And I said, "You are right. But I can point out to you in the case of each one of these sciences what it is a science *of*, this being distinct from the science itself. For instance, the art of calculation, of course, is of the odd and even—how many they are in themselves and with respect to other numbers—isn't that so?"

"Yes indeed," he said.

"Now aren't the odd and even distinct from the art of calculation itself?"

"Of course."

B

"And again, the art of weighing is an art concerned with the heavier and lighter; and the heavy and light are distinct from the art of weighing. Do you agree?"

"Yes, I do."

"Then, since temperance is also a science of something, state what that something is which is distinct from temperance itself."

"This is just what I mean, Socrates," he said. "You arrive at the point of investigating the respect in which temperance differs from all the other sciences, and then you start looking for some way in which it resembles all the others. It's not like this; but rather, all the others are sciences of something else,

C

47. Critias is quite correct in distinguishing the second-order *technē*, temperance, from *technai* of the first order. Socrates does not agree with his distinctions among the latter, however, as he now proceeds to state.

not of themselves, whereas this is the only science which is both of other sciences *and* of itself.[48] And I think you are quite consciously doing what you denied doing a moment ago—you are trying to refute me and ignoring the real question at issue."

"Oh come," I said, "how could you possibly think that even if I were to refute everything you say, I would be doing it for any other reason than the one I would give for a thorough investigation of my own statements—the fear of uncon- 166D sciously thinking I know something when I do not.[49] And this is what I claim to be doing now, examining the argument for my own sake primarily, but perhaps also for the sake of my friends. Or don't you believe it to be for the common good, or for that of most men, that the state of each existing thing should become clear?"

"Very much so, Socrates," he said.

"Pluck up courage then, my friend, and answer the question as seems best to you, paying no attention to whether it is Critias or Socrates who is being refuted. Instead, give your E attention to the argument itself to see what the result of its refutation will be."

"All right, I will do as you say, because you seem to me to be talking sense."

"Then remind me," I asked, "what it is you say about temperance."[50]

"I say," he replied, "that it is the only science that is both a science of itself and of the other sciences."

48. Critias has now understood the distinction between first and second order correctly. But fresh complications arise from his shift from knowledge of self (*heautou*) to knowledge of itself (*heautes*). That is, he has now made temperance its own object instead of giving it a separate object (the self). On the other hand, it could be said that knowledge of the self as temperate is essential to the knowledge of what temperance is.

49. In the *Apology*, Socrates concludes that if he has any wisdom, it consists in not thinking he knows things of which he is ignorant. See 23AB and 29B.

50. The above brief section on method 166CE gives us a rest in preparation for the sustained and difficult argument which now begins. Cf. *Phaedo* 89C-91C.

"Would it then," I said, "also be a science of the absence of science,[51] if it is a science of science?"

"Of course," he said.

167A   "Then only the temperate man will know himself[52] and will be able to examine what he knows and does not know, and in the same way he will be able to inspect other people to see when a man does in fact know what he knows and thinks he knows, and when again he does not know what he thinks he knows, and no one else will be able to do this.[53] And being temperate and temperance and knowing oneself amount to this, to knowing what one knows and does not know. Or isn't this what you say?"

"Yes, it is," he said.

B   "Then for our third libation, the lucky one[54], let us investigate, as though from the beginning, two points: first, whether it is possible or not to know that one knows and does not know what he knows and does not know, and second, should this be perfectly possible, what benefit[55] there would be for those who know this."

"Yes, we ought to look into this," he said.

"Then, come on, Critias," said I, "and consider whether you appear better off than I in these matters, because I am in

51. Socrates introduces this point in order to prepare the way for temperance as the science not only of good but of evil. It is a general principle with Plato that sciences are wholes and that the same person must know both the good and the bad in any field if he is to be an expert in it. See, for instance, *Ion* 531Eff.

52. Note that Socrates has not dropped the idea of self-knowledge involved in temperance.

53. Socrates has given a precise description of his own abilities as they appear in the *Apology*. His mission to the politicians, poets, and artisans depended on his ability to distinguish genuine knowledge from its false conceit. See 21Cff.

54. Literally, "the third [cup] to [Zeus] the Savior". The third cup was regularly drunk to Zeus Soter, especially at the start of a voyage, and became thought of as lucky. Cf. *Republic* 583B and *Philebus* 66D.

55. Should there be no benefit, we shall not have succeeded in defining temperance, since temperance is an admirable (and therefore useful) thing. See below 169B.

difficulties. Shall I tell you where my difficulty lies?"

"Yes, do."

"Well," I said, "wouldn't the whole thing amount to this, if what you said just now is true, that there is one science which is not of anything except itself and the other sciences and that this same science is also a science of the absence of science?"

167C

"Yes indeed."

"Then see what an odd thing we are attempting to say, my friend—because if you look for this same thing in other cases, you will find, I think, that it is impossible."

"How is that, and what cases do you mean?"

"Cases like the following:[56] consider, for instance, if you think there could be a kind of vision that is not the vision of the things that other visions are but is the vision of itself and the other visions and also of the lack of visions, and, although it is a type of vision, it sees no color, only itself and the other visions. Do you think there is something of this kind?"

D

"Good heavens, no, not I."

"And what about a kind of hearing that hears no sound but hears itself and the other hearings and nonhearings?"

"Not this either."

"Then take all the senses together and see if there is any one of them that is a sense of the senses and of itself but that senses nothing which the other senses sense."

"I can't see that there is."

"And do you think there is any desire that is a desire for no pleasure but for itself and the other desires?"

E

"Certainly not."

"Nor indeed any wish, I think, that wishes for no good but only for itself and the other wishes."

56. This exercise in analogy is not to the point since Socrates chooses activities which make no sense when taken as second-order. On this whole section see Thomas G. Rosenmeyer, "Plato and Mass Words," in *Transactions of the American Philological Association* LXXXVIII (1957): 88-102.

"No, that would follow."

"And would you say there was a love of such a sort as to be a love of no fine thing but of itself and the other loves?"

"No," he said, "I would not."

"And have you ever observed a fear that fears itself and the other fears, but of frightful things fears not a one?"

"I have never observed such a thing," he said.

"Or an opinion that is of itself and other opinions but opines nothing that other opinions do?"

"Never."

"But we are saying, it seems, that there is a science of this sort, which is a science of no branch of learning but is a science of itself and the other sciences."

"Yes, we are saying that."

"But isn't it strange if there really is such a thing? However, we ought not yet to state categorically that there is not, but still go on investigating whether there is."[57]

"You are right."

"Come on then: is this science a science of something and does it have a certain faculty of being 'of something'?[58] What about it?"

"Yes, it does."

"And do we say the greater has a certain faculty of being greater than[59] something?"

"Yes, it has."

"Presumably than something less, if it is going to be greater."

"Necessarily."

"Then if we should discover something greater that is greater than the greater things and than itself, but greater than nothing than which the other greater things are greater,

---

57. Notice that the original definition has not been refuted.

58. "Science" is what I have called a "*tinos*-word," that is. See Preface pp. viii-ix.

59. The transition from "science of" to "greater than" makes more sense in Greek than it does in English, since the expression translated "greater than" is, literally, "greater of." Plato investigates the ambiguities of relative terms on a number of occasions, e.g., *Phaedo* 100 Eff. and 102Bff.

surely what would happen to it is that, if it were actually 168C greater than itself, it would also be less than itself, wouldn't it?"

"That would certainly have to be the case, Socrates," he said.

"It would follow, too, that anything that was the double of the other doubles and of itself would, I suppose, be half of itself and of the other doubles—because I don't suppose there is a double of anything else except a half."

"That's true."

"And something that is more than itself will also be less, and the heavier, lighter and the older, younger, and so with all the other cases—the very thing which has its own faculty D applied to itself will have to have that nature towards which the faculty was directed, won't it? I mean something like this: in the case of hearing don't we say that hearing is of nothing else than sound?"

"Yes."

"Then if it actually hears itself, it will hear the sound which it possesses in itself? Because otherwise it would not do any hearing."

"Necessarily so."

"And vision, I take it, O best of men, if it actually sees itself, will have to have some color? Because vision could certainly never see anything that has no color." E

"No, that would follow."

"You observe then, Critias, that of the cases we have gone through, some appear to us to be absolutely impossible, whereas in others it is very doubtful if they could ever apply their own faculties to themselves? And that magnitude and number and similar things belong to the absolutely impossible group, isn't that so?"

"Certainly."

"Again, that hearing or vision or, in fact, any sort of motion should move itself, or heat burn itself—all cases like this also produce disbelief in some, though perhaps there are some in whom it does not. What we need, my friend, is some great 169A

man to give an adequate interpretation of this point in every
detail, whether no existing thing can by nature apply its own
faculty to itself but only towards something else, or whether
some can, but others cannot. We also need him to determine
whether, if there are things that apply to themselves, the science which we call temperance is among them. I do not regard
myself as competent to deal with these matters, and this is
169B why I am neither able to state categorically whether there
might possibly be a science of science nor, if it definitely were
possible, able to accept temperance as such a science before
I investigate whether such a thing would benefit us or not.
Now I divine that temperance is something beneficial and
good. Do you then, O son of Callaeschrus, since the definition
of temperance as the science of science and, more especially,
of the absence of science belongs to you, first clear up this
point, that what I just mentioned is possible and then, after
C having shown its possibility, go on to show that it is useful.
And so, perhaps, you will satisfy me that you are right about
what temperance is."[60]

When Critias heard this and saw that I was in difficulties, then, just as in the case of people who start yawning when
they see other people doing it, he seemed to be affected by
my troubles and to be seized by difficulties himself. But since
his consistently high reputation made him feel ashamed in
the eyes of the company and he did not wish to admit to me
that he was incapable of dealing with the question I had
D asked him, he said nothing clear but concealed his predica-
ment. So I, in order that our argument should go forward,
said, "But if it seems right, Critias, let us now grant this point,
that the existence of a science of science is possible—we can
investigate on some other occasion whether this is really the

60. What Socrates is getting at may perhaps be summed up as follows:
a thing which is "of" something is normally thought to be distinct from
that which it is "of." Thus, if temperance is of itself, it must be distinct
from itself, which appears to be nonsensical. Nevertheless, the truly temperate man would actually possess a consciousness of himself as temperate
(that is, of his own temperance) and there ought to be some way, Plato
thinks, of expressing this phenomenon.

case or not.[61] Come then, if this is perfectly possible, is it any more possible to know what one knows and does not know? We did say, I think, that knowing oneself and being temperate consisted in this?"

"Yes indeed," he said, "and your conclusion seems to me to follow, Socrates, because if a man has a science which knows itself, he would be the very same sort of man as the science which he has.[62] For instance, whenever a person has speed he is swift, and when he has beauty he is beautiful, and when he has knowledge he is knowing. So when a person has a knowledge which knows itself, then I imagine he will be a person who knows himself."

169E

"It is not this point," I said, "on which I am confused, that whenever someone possesses this thing which knows itself he will know himself, but how the person possessing it will necessarily know what he knows and what he does not know."[63]

"But this is the same thing as the other, Socrates."

170A

"Perhaps," I said, "but I'm in danger of being as confused as ever, because I still don't understand how knowing what one knows and does not know is the same thing as knowledge of self."

"How do you mean?" he said.

"It's like this," I said. "Supposing that there is a science of science, will it be anything more than the ability to divide things and say that one is science and the other not?"

"No, it amounts to this."

61. In order to proceed with the discussion Socrates adopts the hypothetical method. See below 172C and *Meno* 86Dff.

62. Note that although Socrates has just said "oneself", Critias continues to say "itself". But as Critias now points out, the difference is really unimportant, since it consists only in the distinction between the quality and the person possessing the quality. (This is a distinction which Plato frequently ignores. Cf. on *Laches* 190E.)

63. Socrates is directing Critias' attention to the part of the definition that stated that temperance is the science, not only of itself, but of the other sciences. Does the consciousness of oneself as temperate extend to the content of these?

"And is it the same thing as the science and absence of
170B science of health, and as the science and absence of science
of justice?"

"Not at all."

"One is medicine, I think, and the other politics, but we
are concerned with science pure and simple."

"What else?"

"Therefore, when a person lacks this additional science
of health and justice but knows science only, seeing that this
is the only knowledge he has, then he will be likely, both in
his own case and in that of others, to know that he knows
something and has a certain science, won't he?"

"Yes."

"And how will he know whatever he knows by this
C   means of science? Because he will know the healthy by medicine, but not by temperance, and the harmonious by music,
but not by temperance, and housebuilding by that art, but not
by temperance, and so on—isn't it so?"

"It seems so."

"But by temperance, if it is merely a science of science,
how will a person know that he knows the healthy or that
he knows housebuilding?"[64]

"He won't at all."

"Then the man ignorant of this won't know *what* he
knows, but only *that* he knows."

"Very likely."

D   "Then this would not be being temperate and would not
be temperance: to know what one knows and does not know,
but only *that* one knows and does not know—or so it seems."

"Probably."

"Nor, when another person claims to know something,
will our friend be able to find out whether he knows what he

---

64. Socrates is bringing out the point that the contents of the first-
order *technai* will be known by these arts and not by an art of the second
order. Plato is faced with the difficult problem of expressing the relationship between conviction of knowledge and awareness of that about which
the conviction is felt.

says he knows or does not know it.[65] But he will only know this much, it seems, that the man has some science; yes, but of what, temperance will fail to inform him."

"Apparently so."

"So neither will he be able to distinguish the man who 170E pretends to be a doctor, but is not, from the man who really is one, nor will he be able to make this distinction for any of the other experts. And let's see what follows: if the temperate man or anyone else whatsoever is going to tell the real doctor from the false, how will he go about it? He won't, I suppose, engage him in conversation on the subject of medicine, because what the doctor knows, we say, is nothing but health and disease, isn't that so?"

"Yes, that is the case."

"But about science the doctor knows nothing, because we have allotted precisely this function to temperance alone."

"Yes."

"Neither will the doctor know anything about medicine since medicine is a science." 171A

"True."

"However, the temperate man will know that the doctor has some science, but in order to try and grasp what sort it is, won't he have to examine what it is of? Because hasn't each science been defined, not just as science, but also by that which it is of?"

"By that, certainly."

"Now medicine is distinguished from the other sciences by virtue of its definition as science of health and disease."

"Yes."

"It follows that the man who wants to examine medicine should look for it where it is to be found, because I don't B suppose he will discover it where it is *not* to be found, do you?"

"Certainly not."

65. The detection of knowledge in others is crucial, since it is the mark of the statesman. (Cf. 171Dff.). In other words, the President of the United States should be able to appoint a competent Secretary of Agriculture without necessarily knowing anything about agriculture himself.

"Then the man who conducts the examination correctly will examine the doctor in those matters in which he is a medical man, namely health and disease."

"So it seems."

"And he will look into the manner of his words and actions to see if what he says is truly spoken and what he does is correctly done?"

"Necessarily."

"But, without the medical art, would anyone be able to follow up either of these things?"

"Certainly not."

171C   "No one, in fact, could do this, it seems, except the doctor—not even the temperate man himself. If he could, he would be a doctor in addition to his temperance."

"That is the case."

"The upshot of the matter is, then, that if temperance is only the science of science and absence of science, the doctor will be able to distinguish neither the man who knows the particulars of his art from the man who does not know them but pretends or supposes he does, nor will he recognize any other genuine practitioner whatsoever, except the man in his own field, the way other craftsmen do."[66]

"It seems so," he said.

D   "Then, Critias," I replied, "what benefit would we get from temperance if it is of this nature? Because if, as we assumed in the beginning, the temperate man knew what he knew and what he did not know (and that he knows the former but not the latter) and were able to investigate another man who was in the same situation, then it would be of the greatest benefit to us to be temperate. Because those of us who had temperance would live lives free from error and so would all those who were under our rule. Neither would we ourselves be attempting to do things we did not understand—rather we would find those who did understand and turn

66. Socrates has pushed the distinction between first- and second-order sciences to its logical conclusion. The upshot, as we now see, is that temperance cannot be beneficial; if so, the definition has failed.

the matter over to them—nor would we trust those over whom we ruled to do anything except what they would do correctly, and this would be that of which they possessed the science. And thus, by means of temperance, every household would be well-run, and every city well-governed,[67] and so in every case where temperance reigned. And with error rooted out and rightness   172A
in control, men so circumstanced would necessarily fare admirably and well in all their doings and, faring well, they would be happy. Isn't this what we mean about temperance, Critias," I said, "when we say what a good thing it would be to know what one knows and what one does not know?"

"This is certainly what we mean," he said.

"But now you see," I replied, "that no science of this sort has put in an appearance."

"I see that," he said.

"Well then," I said, "is this the advantage of the knowl-   B
edge of science and absence of science, which we are now finding out to be temperance—that the man who has this science will learn whatever he learns more easily, and everything will appear to him in a clearer light since, in addition to what he learns, he will perceive the science? And he will examine others on the subjects he himself knows in a more effective fashion, whereas those without the science will conduct their examinations in a weaker and less fruitful way. And are not these, my friend, the kind of benefits we shall reap from   C
temperance? Or are we regarding it as something greater, and demanding that it be greater than it really is?"

"Perhaps that may be so," he said.

"Perhaps," I said, "and perhaps we have been demanding something useless. I say this because certain odd things become clear about temperance if it has this nature. If you are willing, let us investigate the matter by admitting[68] both that it is possible to know a science and also what we assumed temperance to be in the beginning: to know what one knows

67. This is the real point.
68. The hypothetical method again; see 169D above.

172D   and does not know—let us grant this and not deny it. And, having granted all these things, let us investigate more thoroughly whether, if it is like this, it will benefit us in any way. Because what we were saying just now, about temperance being regarded as of great benefit (if it were like this) in the governing of households and cities, does not seem to me, Critias, to have been well said."[69]

"In what way?" he asked.

"Because," I said, "we carelessly agreed that it would be a great good for men if each of us should perform the things he knows and should hand over what he does not know to those others who do."[70]

E   "And weren't we right in agreeing on this?" he said.

"I don't think we were," I replied.

"You certainly say some queer things, Socrates," he said.

"By the dog," I said, "they seem queer to me too, and that is why, when I became aware of this a moment ago, I said that some strange things would come to light and that I was afraid we were not conducting the examination correctly. Because truly, even if there were no doubt that temperance
173A   is like this, it appears in no way clear to me that it does us any good."

"How so?" he said. "Tell me, so that we can both understand what you are saying."

"I think I am making a fool of myself," I said, "but all the same it is necessary to investigate what occurs to us and not to proceed at random, if we are going to have the least care for ourselves."

"You are right," he said.

"Listen then," I said, "to my dream, to see whether it comes through horn or through ivory.[71] If temperance really

---

69. Why? Because we admitted certain things too soon. See Section 169D above.

70. This last has not been precisely stated but is a cardinal point in the *Republic*, e.g. 434Aff. Cf. *Euthydemus* 290BE.

71. The reference is to *Odyssey* XIX, 564—7. True dreams come through the horn gate, deceitful ones through the gate of ivory.

ruled over us and were as we now define it, surely everything would be done according to science: neither would anyone 173B who says he is a pilot (but is not) deceive us, nor would any doctor or general or anyone else pretending to know what he does not know escape our notice. This being the situation, wouldn't we have greater bodily health than we do now, and safety when we are in danger at sea or in battle, and wouldn't we have dishes and all our clothes and shoes and things skill- fully made for us, and many other things as well, because we C would be employing true craftsmen? And, if you will, let us even agree that the mantic art is knowledge of what is to be and that temperance, directing her, keeps away deceivers and sets up the true seers as prophets of the future. I grant that the human race, if thus equipped, would act and live in a scien- D tific way—because temperance, watching over it, would not allow the absence of science to creep in and become our accom- plice. But whether acting scientifically would make us fare well and be happy, this we have yet to learn, my dear Critias."

"But on the other hand," he said, "you will not readily gain the prize of faring well by any other means if you elimi- nate scientific action."

"Instruct me on just one more small point," I said. "When you say that something is scientifically done, are you talking about the science of cutting out shoes?"[72]

"Good heavens no!" E

"Of bronze working, then?"

"Certainly not."

"Then of wool or wood or some similar thing?"

"Of course not."

"Then," I said, "we no longer keep to the statement that the man who lives scientifically is happy. Because those who live in the ways we mentioned are not admitted by you to be happy, but rather you seem to me to define the happy man as one who lives scientifically concerning certain specific things.

---

72. As soon as Socrates begins to argue in terms of first-order arts, we can expect trouble. Cf. 170Cff.

And perhaps you mean the person I mentioned a moment ago, the man who knows what all future events will be, namely the

174A seer.[73] Are you referring to this man or some other?"

"Both to this one," he said, "and another."

"Which one?" I said. "Isn't it the sort of man who, in addition to the future, knows everything that has been and is now and is ignorant of nothing? Let us postulate the existence of such a man. Of this man I think you would say that there was no one living who was more scientific."[74]

"Certainly not."

"There is one additional thing I want to know: which one of the sciences makes him happy? Do all of them do this equally?"

"No, very unequally," he said.

B "Well, which one in particular makes him happy? The one by which he knows which one of the things are and have been and are to come? Will it be the one by which he knows checker playing?"

"Oh for heaven's sake," he said.

"Well, the one by which he knows calculation?"

"Of course not."

"Well, will it be that by which he knows health?"

"That's better," he said.

"But the most likely case," I said, "is that by which he knows what?"

"By which he knows good," he said, "and evil."[75]

"You wretch," said I, "all this time you've been leading me right round in a circle[76] and concealing from me that it was

---

73. Cf. *Laches* 195E.

74. Cf. *Laches* 198Dff. and, especially, 199D.

75. Socrates finally gets the answer he wants. What Plato appears to be getting at is that since the first-order arts are ruled by one of the second order, they will derive their character from the latter. They cannot make us happy (in spite of continuing to perform their normal functions) unless the ruling second-order art is one to make us happy. But if this ruling art should turn out to be the science of good and evil, the requisite happiness is forthcoming.

76. Probably Socrates means that Critias has led him back to "the doing of good things" of 163E.

not living scientifically that was making us fare well and be 174C
happy, even if we possessed all the sciences put together, but
that we have to have this one science of good and evil. Because, Critias, if you consent to take away this science from
the other sciences, will medicine any the less produce health,
or cobbling produce shoes, or the art of weaving produce
clothes, or will the pilot's art any the less prevent us from
dying at sea or the general's art in war?"

"They will do it just the same," he said.

"But my dear Critias, our chance of getting any of these
things well and beneficially done will have vanished if this is D
lacking."

"You are right."

"Then this science, at any rate, is not temperance, but
that one of which the function is to benefit us. And it is not a
science of science and absence of science but of good and
evil. So that, if this latter one is beneficial, temperance would
be something else for us."

"But why should not this be beneficial?" he said. "Because if temperance really is a science of sciences and rules
over the other sciences, then I suppose it would rule over E
this science of the good and would benefit us."[77]

"And would this science make us healthy," I said, "and
not the art of medicine?[78] And would it perform the tasks of
the other arts rather than each of them performing its own
task? Didn't we protest solemnly just a moment ago that it is
a science of science and absence of science only and of nothing
else? We did, didn't we?"

"It seems so, at any rate."

"Then it will not be the craftsman of health?"

"Certainly not."

77. Critias has asked the right question (why should not temperance
be beneficial) but gives the wrong answer. That is, he envisages temperance (a second-order art), ruling over the first-order arts plus the second-
order art (science) of good and evil. The answer to the problem (and
the one which Plato I think intended) is to equate the two second-order
arts. In other words, temperance *is* the science of good and evil.

78. Socrates reverts once more to the first-order arts.

175A   "Because health belonged to some other art, didn't it?"
"Yes, to another."
"Then it will be of no use, my friend. Because we have just awarded this work to another art, isn't that so?"
"Yes indeed."
"Then how will temperance be useful when it is the craftsman of no useful thing?"[79]
"Apparently it won't be any use at all, Socrates."
"You see then, Critias, that my earlier fears were reasonable and that I was right to blame myself for discerning nothing useful in temperance? Because I don't suppose that the
B   thing we have agreed to be the finest of all would have turned out to be useless if I had been of any use in making a good search. But now we have got the worst of it in every way and are unable to discover to which one of existing things the lawgiver[80] gave this name, temperance. Furthermore, we gave our joint assent to many things which did not follow from our argument.[81] For instance, we conceded that there was a science of science when the argument did not allow us to make this statement. Again, we conceded that this science knew the tasks of the other sciences, when the argument did not allow us to say this either, so that our temperate man should turn out to be knowing, both that he knows things he knows and
C   does not know things he does not know.[82] And we made this concession in the most prodigal manner, quite overlooking the impossibility that a person should in some fashion know what he does not know at all—because our agreement amounts to saying he knows things he does not know. And yet,

79. This is not, of course, an insuperable difficulty; we should not by now expect a second-order art to have a first-order product.
80. This is the nomothete of *Cratylus* 388E and *passim*.
81. Socrates recalls the assumptions which were made on hypothesis. See 169D and 172C.
82. But this is precisely what Socratic wisdom is, to be aware of one's own ignorance. It should be noted, too, that Plato here takes exception to the strict opposition between knowing and not-knowing, which is fundamental to a number of the Parmenidean fallacies exposed in the *Euthydemus*. (E.g., 293Bff.)

I think, there could be nothing more irrational than this. But in spite of the fact that the inquiry has shown us to be both complacent and easy, it is not a whit more capable of discovering the truth. It has, in fact, made fun of the truth to this extent, that it has very insolently exposed as useless the definition of temperance which we agreed upon and invented earlier. I am not so much vexed on my own account, but on yours, Charmides," I said, "I am very vexed indeed, if, with such a body and, in addition, a most temperate soul, you should derive no benefit from this temperance nor should it be of any use to you in this present life.[83] And I am still more vexed on behalf of the charm I took so much trouble to learn from the Thracian, if it should turn out to be worthless. I really do not believe this to be the case; rather I think that I am a worthless inquirer. Because I think that temperance is a great good, and if you truly have it, that you are blessed.[84] So see whether you do have it and are in no need of the charm—because if you do have it, my advice to you would rather be to regard me as a babbler, incapable of finding out anything whatsoever by means of argument, and yourself as being exactly as happy as you are temperate."

175D

E

176A

And Charmides said, "But good heavens, Socrates, I don't know whether I have it or whether I don't—because how would I know the nature of a thing when neither you nor Critias is able to discover it, as you say? However, I don't really believe you, Socrates, but I think I am very much in need of the charm, and as far as I am concerned I am willing to be charmed by you every day until you say I have had enough."

B

"Very well, Charmides," said Critias, "if you do this, it will convince me of your temperance—if you submit yourself

83. Plato's readers could hardly fail to be reminded here of what Charmides ultimately became. We should note also that, since Charmides failed to define temperance, he did not, presumably, possess it in the first place. See 159A.

84. Perhaps a hint that the equation of temperance with the science of good and evil is correct. Note also that it is not the charm (the *logos*) which has turned out to be worthless, only Socrates. Cf. 166E.

to be charmed by Socrates and let nothing great or small dissuade you from it."

"This is the course I shall follow," he said, "and I shall not give it up. I would be acting badly if I failed to obey my guardian and did not carry out your commands."

176C

"Well then," said Critias, "these are my instructions."

"And I shall execute them," he said, "from this day forward."

"Look here," I said, "what are you two plotting?"

"Nothing," said Charmides—"our plotting is all done."

"Are you going to use force," I asked, "and don't I get a preliminary hearing?"

"We shall have to use force," said Charmides, "seeing that this fellow here has given me my orders. So you had better take counsel as to your own procedure."

D

"What use is counsel?" said I. "Because when you undertake to do anything by force, no man living can oppose you."

"Well then," he said, "don't oppose me."

"Very well, I shan't," said I.[85]

---

85. Charmides seems to have benefited from the discussion to some extent. Yet he is still inclined—under the influence of Critias?—to use force to get what he wants. (Cf. the initial hint of this at 156A.) Again Plato probably intends to remind his readers of what Charmides would become.

Index